WHAT THE CRITICS SAY:

A very worthwhile addition to any travel library. —**WCBS Newsradio**

Armed with these guides, you may never again stay in a conventional hotel.
—**Travelore Report**

Easily carried ... neatly organized ... wonderful. A helpful addition to my travel library. The authors wax as enthusiastically as I do about the almost too-quaint-to-believe Country Inns. —**San Francisco Chronicle**

One can only welcome such guide books and wish them long, happy, and healthy lives in print. —**Wichita Kansas Eagle**

This series of pocket-sized paperbacks will guide travelers to hundreds of little known and out of the way inns, lodges, and historic hotels.... a thorough menu.
—**(House Beautiful's) Colonial Homes**

Charming, extremely informative, clear and easy to read; excellent travelling companions. —**Books-Across-The-Sea** *(The English Speaking Union)*

...a fine selection of inviting places to stay... provide excellent guidance....
—**Blair & Ketchum's Country Journal**

Obviously designed for our kind of travel.... [the authors] have our kind of taste.
—**Daily Oklahoman**

The first guidebook was so successful that they have now taken on the whole nation.... Inns are chosen for charm, architectural style, location, furnishings and history. —**Portland Oregonian**

Many quaint and comfy country inns throughout the United States... The authors have a grasp of history and legend. —**Dallas (Tx.) News**

Very fine travel guides. —**Santa Ana (Calif.) Register**

A wonderful source for planning trips. —**Northampton (Mass.) Gazette**

...pocketsize books full of facts.... attractively made and illustrated.
—**New York Times Book Review**

Hundreds of lovely country inns reflecting the charm and hospitality of various areas throughout the U.S. —**Youngstown (Ohio) Vindicator**

Some genius must have measured the average American dashboard, because the Compleat Traveler's Companions fit right between the tissues and bananas on our last trip.... These are good-looking books with good-looking photographs.... very useful.

—**East Hampton (N.Y.) Star**

ALSO AVAILABLE IN THE COMPLEAT TRAVELER SERIES

☐ *George Ferguson's* Europe by Eurail

☐ *George Ferguson's* Britain by Britrail

☐ The Total Traveler by Ship *(Ethel Blum)*

☐ Country Inns & Historic Hotels of Great Britain

☐ Country Inns & Historic Hotels of Canada

☐ Country Inns & Historic Hotels of Ireland

☐ Country New England Inns

☐ Country Inns & Historic Hotels of the Middle Atlantic States

☐ Country Inns & Historic Hotels of the South

☐ Country Inns & Historic Hotels of the Midwest & Rocky
    Mountain States

☐ Country Inns & Historic Hotels of California and the West

☐ Country New England Historical & Sightseeing Guide

☐ Country New England Antiques, Crafts, & Factory Outlets

☐ Guide to California and the Pacific Northwest

☐ Guide to the Southwest

☐ Guide to the South

If your local bookseller, gift shop, or country inn does not stock a particular title, ask them to order directly from Burt Franklin & Co., Inc., 235 East 44th Street, New York, New York 10017, U.S.A. Telephone orders are accepted from recognized retailers and credit card holders. In the United States, call 212-687-5250 during regular business hours.

COUNTRY INNS

Lodges, and Historic Hotels of the

Midwest and Rocky Mountain States

by

Anthony Hitchcock

and

Jean Lindgren

BURT FRANKLIN & CO.

Published by Burt Franklin & Company
235 East Forty-fourth Street
New York, New York 10017

Copyright © 1979, 1980, 1981 by Burt Franklin & Co., Inc.

Library of Congress Cataloging in Publication Data

Hitchcock, Anthony
Country inns, lodges, and historic hotels of the
Midwest and Rocky Mountain States

(The Compleat traveler's companion)
Includes index.
1. Hotels, taverns, etc.—Middle West—Directories.
2. Hotels, taverns, etc.—Rocky Mountains region—
Directories. I. Lindgren, Jean, joint author.
II. Title.   III. Series: Compleat traveler's
companion.
TX907.H5392   1981   647'.947701   80–29536
ISBN 0-89102-210-4

Manufactured in the United States of America
1 3 4 2

Contents

INTRODUCTION   VII

MAPS   X

THE GREAT LAKES REGION

ILLINOIS   1

    Brussells • Eldred • Galena • Grand Detour • Nauvoo

INDIANA   14

    Angola • Batesville • Mitchell • New Harmony

MICHIGAN   22

    Bay View • Dearborn • Farmington Hills • Harbor Springs • Mackinac Island • Marshall • Saint Clair

MINNESOTA   38

    Grand Marais • New Prague • Sauk Centre • Stillwater • Wabasha

OHIO   51

    Granville • Lebanon

WISCONSIN   57

    Bayfield • Ellison Bay • Fish Creek • Green Lake • Lewis • Madeline • Poynette • Sister Bay • Sturgeon Bay

THE CENTRAL STATES

IOWA   77
    Keosauqua • Homestead • Mount Pleasant

KANSAS   83
    Ashland • Beaumont • Harper

MISSOURI   89
    Hollister • Sainte Genevieve

NEBRASKA   93
    Belgrade • Crawford

NORTH DAKOTA   97
    Fargo • Medora

SOUTH DAKOTA   101
    Canova • Custer State Park • Hill City

THE EASTERN ROCKIES

COLORADO   106
    Boulder • Colorado Springs • Creede • Cripple Creek
    • Del Norte • Durango • Empire • Green Mountain Falls
    • Ouray • Redstone • Silverton • Telluride

IDAHO   132
    Mountain Home • North Fork • Priest Lake • Salmon

MONTANA   139
    Big Sky • Essex • Glacier National Park

WYOMING   154
    Atlantic City • Cody • Evanston • Grand Teton National
    Park • Medicine Bow • Moran • Saratoga • Shoshone
    National Forest • Wapiti • Yellowstone National Park

INDEX OF INNS, WITH RATES AND CHARGE CARDS   177

Introduction

W E CONFESS to having a love affair with the Midwest and the Rockies. It has been a long time coming. As confirmed Easterners, we had looked up and down both coasts wearing blinders against the many wonders of the central part of the country. To our delight we have turned up historic hotels and lovely old inns in every state from Michigan to Colorado. As one progresses from east to west, the trend starts with country inns, many surviving from the stagecoach days, and then changes to the restored early hotels and lodges of the Rocky Mountains. In some states, notably Ohio, restoration has followed a tendency to establish fine country dining places, without lodgings, in old taverns.

The diversity of terrain included in the pages of this guide is as great as the country has to offer—from waving fields of wheat to the towering peaks of the Rocky Mountains. Although parts of the Midwest remain somewhat off the beaten track during the harsh winter months, the northern states of this region and, of course, states like Colorado and Idaho have skiing seasons that are long and filled with the excitement of the finest skiing on the continent. The vastest wilderness areas of the country and, therefore, its finest state and national parks are within the boundaries of the states included here.

It must be noted that many of the fine early inns and hotels in this region suffered more than in other parts of the country from a rush of enthusiasm for "modernization" in the face of competition from encroaching motels. Moreover, there has been a somewhat slower restoration movement throughout the Midwest. So we have, on occasion, compromised our "purist" feelings for authentic restoration and included a number of historic buildings that have such modern touches as imitation paneling and "drop" ceilings. Despite the tendency for the decor to offend our sense of authenticity, we feel that many of these fine smaller inns and hotels provide pleasing alternatives to the accommodations of most motels.

We suggest that you write early for literature about inns that you have chosen as interesting. Read the brochures, look at the pictures, check the maps, and determine if the inns will actually meet your needs. Inns are not at all like motels. Each has its special qualities that can be one's personal pleasure, but not necessarily another's. Do not hesitate to call an innkeeper and discuss your requirements. In fact, we feel that for us this is the most important thing to do before making a reservation. Country inns are a reflection of the syle and personality of the innkeeper. More than in a motel or large hotel, the personal ambience is likely to affect your visit. Most innkeepers are highly understanding of the needs of their guests. If you are seeking an old-fashioned, small country inn secluded from most outside distractions, ask before you go. We have purposely included a wide range of inns, lodges, historic hotels, and small resorts.

We have quoted the most recent room rates in a combined rate chart and index at the end of the book. Readers should note that the listed rates are *subject to change*. While the quoted rates are for double occupancy in most cases, single travelers as well as larger groups should inquire about special rates. We list daily room rates as based on the American Plan (AP, all three meals included), Modified American Plan (MAP, breakfast and dinner included), or European Plan (EP, no meals or a light Continental breakfast only). In many cases a tax and a service charge will be added. Be sure to ask. Children and pets present special problems for many inns. If either is *not* welcome at an inn it is noted in the description. These regulations also often change, and it is imperative that families traveling with either inquire in advance. Even though many inns state they are open all year, we find that many of these close during slow periods. Call first to confirm your room reservations.

We suggest that before traveling to any state you write to its department of travel and tourism. Ask for the state road map and a packet of general travel information. If you have special travel interests or needs, the department can often send special pamphlets or hints. In the pages that follow, readers will discover that the material is organized by region and, within each region, by state. Within each state, listings are alphabetical by the names of the towns and villages. For those seeking a particular inn, there is an index at the end of the book, which also contains rate and credit-card information.

The inns in this book were chosen for their inherent charm, based partially on their architectural style, location, furnishings, and history. We used no strict definition of an inn in selecting places for inclusion. Though the term "inn" usually means a place with both lodging and food, we have listed several that provide no meals. We find, in some cases, that the food operation actually is so dominant as to detract from the quiet and charm of a place. We did not include any old inns that serve meals only, although a great many exist in the Midwest.

The information incorporated here came from several sources: our personal knowledge of the inns, recommendations of others we deem reliable, and personal surveys of innkeepers. We have made every effort to provide information as carefully and accurately as possible, but remind readers that all rates and schedules are subject to change. Finally, we have neither solicited nor accepted fees or gratuities for inclusion in this book or in any other book in the Compleat Traveler Series.

We would like this book to continue to grow in usefulness in succeeding editions. In order to make this possible we appreciate suggestions from our readers. We very much wish to hear of your experiences at the inns listed in this volume and receive your suggestions for future volumes. We shall make every effort to answer all letters personally. Please write to us in care of our publishers: Burt Franklin and Co., 235 East Forty-fourth Street, New York, NY 10017.

Have a good trip!

JEAN LINDGREN
ANTHONY HITCHCOCK

THE GREAT LAKES REGION

Map by Ira Kennedy

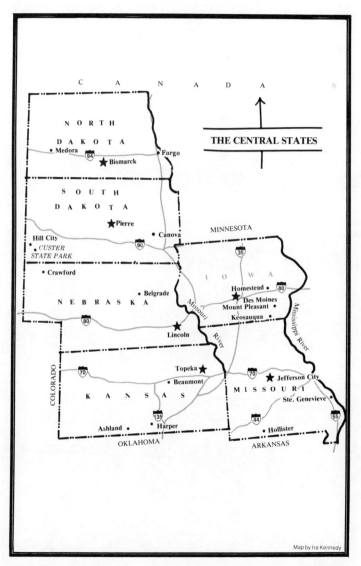

THE CENTRAL STATES

CANADA

NORTH DAKOTA
• Medora 94 ★ Bismarck • Fargo

SOUTH DAKOTA
★ Pierre 90 • Canova

MINNESOTA

Hill City •
• CUSTER STATE PARK

• Crawford

IOWA 35

NEBRASKA • Belgrade Homestead • 80
★ Des Moines
Mount Pleasant •
Keosauqua •

80 Missouri

★ Lincoln River

Mississippi River

COLORADO 70 Topeka ★ 70 ★ Jefferson City 55
• Beaumont MISSOURI Ste. Genevieve •

KANSAS 135 44

Ashland • • Harper • Hollister

OKLAHOMA ARKANSAS

Map by Ira Kennedy

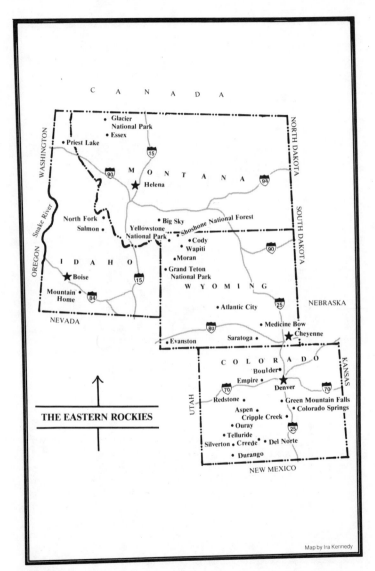

THE EASTERN ROCKIES

Map by Ira Kennedy

Illinois

WITTMOND HOTEL

Brussells, IL 62013. 618-883-2345. *Innkeeper:* Carl H. Wittmond.
Open all year.

The historic Wittmond Hotel sits at the foot of Calhoun County between the Mississippi and Illinois rivers, near the point where the Illinois joins the mighty Mississippi on its way to the gulf. The dark red building has white trim and a long, narrow second-floor veranda across the entire front of the hotel. The original inn was constructed in 1847, with additions several years later. It was a former stagecoach stop in the historic French colonial district. Years ago the inn served mainly traveling salesmen, and the restaurant existed to feed them. The hotel made additional money from the bar and several little shops housed under its roof. The old General Store is still in business here today, and Mr. Wittmond runs an antique shop in another.

Mr. Carl Wittmond, one of the most pleasant innkeepers guests are likely to encounter anywhere, "retired" here to run his hotel after some twelve years as an Illinois state legislator. He was instrumental in getting a free ferry in operation from Pere Marquette State Park across the Illinois River to Calhoun County near Brussells. Summer weekends bring hundreds of people to the famed dinners served at the hotel restaurant. Weekend visits here require booking several weeks in advance. Other times of the week and other seasons are peaceful, and guests have a chance to meet and chat with the innkeeper.

The inn's guest rooms are furnished eclectically according to the whims of Mr. Wittmond. He believes a person should buy what appeals to him and not worry whether it all blends together. The rooms contain a combination of original antique hotel furnishings

and newer pieces of the Wittmond family collections. The bedrooms are clean, comfortable, and cozy—three important hotel "c's." There is a lounge for guests, but the favorite spot seems to be the Wittmond Bar, a down-home country place where families come, kids and all, for an afternoon of visiting and card playing with visitors and local residents.

Family-style meals are served daily in the old-fashioned dining room. Because Calhoun County is real "apple country," meals feature apples in a variety of ways. A Lazy Susan filled with apple rings, peach preserves, corn relish, and raw vegetable sticks starts the meal. The second course is plates of the hotel's own homemade sausage with side dishes of coleslaw and apple sauce. Everyone gets a steaming bowl of homemade soup. The main course is a hearty dish of the day, such as fried Illinois chicken, roast beef, or perhaps country ham or pork with accompanying fresh peas, corn, green beans, potatoes, or whatever is in season, along with hot rolls.

Accommodations: 13 rooms, 4 with private bath. *Driving Instructions:* The best way to get to Brussells is to go north on the Great River Road out of Alton. Alton is north of Saint Louis, Missouri, on the other side of the Mississippi River. Take Great River Road along the Mississippi to the town of Grafton and Pere Marquette State Park. From there take the free ferry across to Calhoun County and Brussells. When the river freezes over there is really no good way to get to the hotel. However, it is open all year, so if you figure out a way, by all means go.

HOBSON'S BLUFFDALE

Eldred-Hillview Road, Eldred, Illinois. Mailing address: Route 1, Eldred, IL 62027. 217-983-2854. *Innkeepers:* Bill and Lindy Hobson. Open May through October.

Bill Hobson's great-great-grandfather John Russell bought the land for Hobson's farm from the U.S. Government in 1818. Russell, an author whose poems appeared in *McGuffy's Fifth Reader*, built the Federalist-Georgian farmhouse ten years later from native limestone quarried from the nearby river bluffs. The walls are 2 feet thick and the house has six fireplaces, originally the only source of heat. John Russell, a great admirer of Charles Dickens, corresponded with him for many years. When Dickens was touring America he was a guest at Bluffdale. Great-great-grandmother Russell had very strong anti-slavery convictions. Sometime before the Civil War someone came to the farm bearing a petition to make Illinois a slave state. He handed the petition to Grandmother Russell as she sat before the huge fireplace in her kitchen. She read the words and gazed thoughtfully at the long list of names supporting its tenets, then silently, dropped the petition behind the blazing backlog.

Today, this fireplace, large enough to cook a deer or small steer in, is a dominant feature of the sitting room. When the Hobsons moved into the house (seven generations of Bill's family have now lived there) they found it barely livable by modern standards, and their first efforts were to restore and modernize it. In the process they discovered four walled-up fireplaces upstairs. They added plumbing and a new electrical system, made major improvements to the farm buildings, and built a two-story addition to the house. Finally, as the guest business blossomed at Bluffdale, they built a separate gambrel-roofed "bunkhouse" containing air-conditioned guest rooms and suites that can sleep up to seven.

Lindy and her family start early each day to prepare the three meals served to guests. Working in her large kitchen, she turns out quantities of fine farm cooking. She is particularly proud of her fried chicken, barbecued whole pork, pot roast, and barbecued pork chops. Meals are accompanied by farm-baked breads, sweet rolls, and pies or cakes. In the morning the generous farm breakfast includes sausage and bacon made at Bluffdale. Guests who wish to eat lunch while hiking in the surrounding woods are supplied with picnic lunches.

Bluffdale is a fully operating farm that raises pigs, chickens, sheep, and horses. There is a farrowing house where the baby pigs are born, and the farm usually has pigs at several stages of growth. Guests who wish to understand the entire pig-raising process from beginning to end are welcome to accompany the Hobsons when they take the hogs to market. Most, however, are happy to enjoy the farm activities at Bluffdale and enjoy the surrounding bluffs and hiking trails. The farm has a heated swimming pool, and the local creeks and the Illinois River provide fishing opportunities. The Hobsons frequently hold outdoor barbecues and hot dog roasts; square dancing and table tennis are offered in the recreation room. Horseback riding is available over paths that crisscross the 200 acres of the farm, and pony-cart rides are available for the younger children who are guests.

Accommodations: 5 rooms and 3 two-room suites with private bath. *Pets:* Not permitted. *Driving Instructions:* Take Route 108 to Eldred. The farm is 3½ miles north on the Eldred-Hillview Road.

Galena, Illinois

COLONIAL GUEST HOUSE

1004 Park Avenue, Galena, IL 61036. 815-777-0336. *Innkeeper:* Mrs. Roy Keller. Open all year.

The Colonial Guest House, a big Greek Revival built in 1826, is on a hill overlooking historic Galena and a river of the same name. The house is quite near the Eastend Bridge over the Galena River; this river was at one time as wide and as deep as the Mississippi, but plowing and erosion of the farmlands to the north have filled it in considerably. The guest house has many porches. The tall pillars and trim are painted white against the deep red of the house itself. Mrs. Keller, the innkeeper, is an avid antique collector and runs her shop, the Carriage House, out of the pillared side rooms of the Colonial. Many of her choicest finds end up in the large rooms of this gracious home. Guests here are likely to be taken with the crystal chandeliers, Oriental rugs, ornate mirrors, and velvet-cushioned furniture. Most of the rooms are open to guests, making them feel at home immedi-

ately. Many marble fireplaces are in evidence in the living quarters and guest rooms but are not used because of the expense and bother of hauling wood in and out.

Bedrooms have period wallpapers and 11-foot ceilings, antique furniture and Oriental rugs, mirrors, and velvet-cushioned chairs and sofas. The private bathrooms contain clawfoot tubs that can hold great quantities of hot water.

Mrs. Keller will gladly recommend nearby Galena restaurants for lunches and dinners. In warm weather it is pleasant to take a cup of coffee to one of the 8- by 36-foot porches and relax and enjoy the scenery. The Colonial has six of these porches, two reserved for guests' use. The house is in a strategic location, one of the favorite spots of artists and photographers.

Accommodations: 4 rooms with private bath. *Pets:* Small, well-behaved pets are permitted. *Driving Instructions:* The house is near the corner of Park Avenue and Decatur Street in Galena. Decatur Street is Routes 20 and 84 and crosses the bridge over the river into the main part of town just in front of the guest house.

STILLMAN MANOR
513 Bouthillier Street, Galena, IL 61036. 815-777-0557. *Innkeepers:* Marilyn Jensen and Merlin Camon. Open all year.

Stillman Manor is a fine example of the architecture of Galena. The mansion was built in 1858 by General Stillman, a close friend and associate of Ulysses S. Grant's. The Grant home, a historic site, is just 200 yards below the Manor. The Stillman Manor and Grant's home are the only two mansions on this hill, and they sit, respectively, at and near the top. The Stillman Manor has a widow's walk, a favorite spot for artists and lovers, overlooking the town below. After the Civil War, General Stillman ran a very successful business, and his larder was always full. General Grant was not so fortunate, although his home had been built for him by grateful citizens. Grant and several of his generals were frequently Stillman's dinner guests in the room now called the General's Room, which features a large fireplace, portraits of all of Grant's generals, and a Waterford chandelier. The inn is furnished throughout with Victorian antiques blending with the large, high-ceilinged rooms, tall windows, and ornate fireplaces.

A wide staircase leads to the guest rooms, which are furnished in

the style of the nineteenth century. There are tall armoirs, massive walnut-headboard beds, and companion pieces. Four rooms are enhanced by fireplaces with ornate marble or wood mantels. Their hearths have been converted to house gas-burning fireplaces. Above the guests' quarters is the widow's walk, and behind that a flat deck where painters, photographers, and sunbathers enjoy the sun and the view of Galena.

The dining room walls of exposed natural stone form a backdrop to gold tablecloths and blue velvet chairs, seventeen of which came from Chicago's famous Pump Room. Adjacent is a wide expanse of brick patio with umbrella-shaded tables where guests may dine in warm weather. Cocktails and wine are served in the Rathskeller, a miniature dungeon with dark stone walls and low ceilings.

One unusual feature of dining at the manor is the Medieval banquet held weekends. The evening includes authentic costuming, handmade dishes patterned after authentic period service, strolling minstrels, and a lord mayor as master of ceremonies. Banquets last more than three hours and involve an appropriately large number of "removes" or courses.

In winter the dining rooms are open only on Mondays, Fridays, and Saturdays.

Accommodations: 7 rooms with private bath. *Pets:* Not permitted. *Driving Instructions:* The Stillman Manor is 200 yards above the Ulysses S. Grant home, a historic site that is well marked. The Manor is on Bouthillier Street at the crest of the hill. The street is off Routes 20 and 84 (Decatur Street), across the river from the town's business section.

THE VICTORIAN MANSION GUEST HOUSE
301 South High Street, Galena, IL 61036. 815-777-0675. *Innkeepers:* Charles and Linda Primrose. Open all year.

The Victorian Mansion is a seventeen-room Italianate home built in 1861 by Augustus Estey, a wealthy lead smelter and banker. In the prosperous mining days the mansion was frequently the scene of parties that welcomed prestigious visitors to Galena, including Ulysses Grant. The Grant family reciprocated after their visit by having the Estey daughter spend the winter with them at the White House. Built on rock on a knoll overlooking Galena, the mansion has walls of 12-inch brick, and the woodwork and fireplaces are original. There is a three-story brick coachhouse on the grounds, as well as the chimney and fireplace of an earlier building that served as the Estey home until the mansion was completed. The grounds include more than 2 acres of large shade trees.

When the Primrose family moved to Galena, the mansion had been in use for about twenty-five years as a somewhat neglected guest house. The Primroses brought with them their collection of Victorian furniture and installed it (with many additions) in the original bedrooms, which they fully refurbished and restored. As you enter the house, you pass through a double entryway with a large secretary and a Victorian hatrack in the alcove. In the hall stands a 10-foot-tall grandfather clock, which has clearance to spare thanks to the high ceilings that are the rule in the mansion. Before you is the commanding oval staircase that spirals up to the third floor.

All guest rooms are on the second floor; three connect and once served as the master bedroom suite. Another was originally the nursery for the Estey family and is directly above the mansion's kitchen, where servants could hear the baby crying and come upstairs to comfort it. This room, which contains a brass bed, marble-top dresser and

commode, and a love seat, is usually selected by honeymooning couples, of which an average of two a week come to the mansion. The room's large kerosine-lamp hanging chandelier, recently electrified, has yellow shades and is decorated with an intricate bird made of inlaid silver and green jewels. Hanging from the lamp are more than a hundred prisms. The walls in this room, as in all the guest rooms, are papered with Victorian prints set in "picture framing" with painted walls above. The other guest rooms have similar period lighting, some converted kerosene chandeliers and others converted gas lamps. All rooms have *Gone with the Wind* reproduction lamps on the desks or bedside tables. Several rooms have heavy carved walnut bedroom sets that include 8-foot-6-inch tall bedsteads with matching bureaus and commodes. Carpeting in the guest rooms is either original Oriental rugs or reproductions by Karastan. The woodwork throughout the mansion is hand-grained pine that was prepared to resemble oak trim and paneling. Charles and Linda are considered to be among the most knowledgeable local people about the attractions of Galena. They take pride in being part of a friendly small town and will be happy to introduce "city folk" to their community.

Accommodations: 6 rooms; 1 with private bath, 5 sharing 2 baths. *Pets:* Not permitted. *Driving Instructions:* Take U.S. 20 east from Dubuque or west from Rockford to the center of Galena.

Grand Detour, Illinois

COLONIAL INN

Rock and Green Streets, Grand Detour, Illinois. Mailing address: Route 3, Dixon, IL 61021. 815-652-4422. *Innkeeper:* James W. Pufall. Open all year.

The Colonial Inn, built as a private residence by a local businessman, Solon Cumins, was constructed along classic Italianate lines. The big brick building was converted to a hotel before the turn of the century and remains so eighty years later. The adjoining estates are homes on spacious grounds. It is on 2½ acres of landscaped lawns shaded by many tall trees. The Colonial Inn is owned and run by James Pufall, who has augmented the remaining original furnishings of this Victorian estate with his own collection of antiques and near antiques. A visit to this inn and the town is like a trip back in time to the gracious era of the nineteenth century. The ground-floor rooms, including the parlor, have floor-to-ceiling windows shaded by the white-pillared porch. The furnishings and décor throughout the inn are primarily Victorian, with a smattering of earlier antiques. Most of the rooms have the original fireplaces, once the only sources of heat but now merely decorative.

Guest rooms are individually decorated in the styles of the period. Some are painted with the true Victorian colors, others have antique and reproduction wallpapers. Half the rooms have 12-foot ceilings, and the rest muddle through under 9-footers. Air conditioning and private baths are available with some of the rooms. Although the night air is cool and fresh even in the hottest months, some people prefer air conditioning. Be sure to say so if you are one of them. Three old-fashioned hall bathrooms are also provided.

Meals are not served at the Colonial, but Mr. Pufall will gladly recommend several places nearby on the river and in neighboring towns.

Accommodations: 12 rooms, 4 with private bath. *Pets:* Not permitted. *Driving Instructions:* The inn is 5 miles north of Dixon off Route 2, and 35 miles south of Rockford off Route 2. Look for Rock Street in the village and go west three blocks. (Route 2 runs north and south.) The East-West Tollway, Route 5, is just below Dixon. Take Route 26 to Dixon and Route 2 at the arch north to Grand Detour.

Nauvoo, Illinois

Nauvoo is a fascinating town historically. On a scenic bluff above a crescent curve in the Mississippi, it overlooks hundreds of acres of farmland that stretch out past the river to the terraced hills beyond, and it is famed for its scenic beauty. But it is even more famous nationwide as the turbulent home of the Mormons in the mid-nineteenth century. Joseph Smith and his followers settled in Nauvoo, built many homes, and started their great temple here. Persecutions of the religious sect led to the arrest, jailing, and murder of Smith and his brother. Brigham Young led many of the people out of strife-torn Nauvoo and on to Utah. Later, French Icarians tried to establish their form of communal living here. It failed, but they did manage to begin a profitable wine and cheese-making industry in Nauvoo that flourishes today. A great many historic Mormon buildings still stand, and a number of them are open to the public. A good start to a tour of the town is a trip to the Nauvoo Restoration Visitor Center on North Main Street. It has movies, exhibits, and informational guides.

HOTEL NAUVOO

Route 96, Town Center, Nauvoo, IL 62354. 217-453-2211. *Innkeeper:* Elmer Kraus. Open April through October.

Hotel Nauvoo, a landmark in this early Mormon town, began as a private residence in 1840. Its architecture is strongly pioneer Mormon —it was built during the turbulent Mormon period in Nauvoo—with attractive porches, verandas, and a large cupola. The home opened its doors to travelers in the 1880s. The Kraus family bought the hotel in 1946 and began its extensive restoration. Several new kitchens were added, and a large dining addition went up in the 1960s. This room, the Nauvoo Room, was constructed of old handmade bricks from a building that had been torn down on the property. The brickmaker's fingerprints can still be seen in the walls. The room is dedicated to the late Lane K. Newbury, the artist who designed it and whose paintings hang throughout the hotel. Each of several other dining rooms in the hotel has the handcarved woodwork and arches characteristic of the old home.

The Hotel Nauvoo is a very popular place to dine; the many specialties are offered with wines from the local winery and blue

cheeses produced in town. Meals are family-style; each diner is served an entreé and then helps himself to the big bowls of fresh vegetables, potatoes, and the hotel's famous wild rice dressing. House specialties are channel catfish, barbecued ribs, and home-baked turkey. Dinners come with plenty of fresh rolls, blueberry muffins, and Nauvoo Concord grape jelly. Dessert is a dish of homemade vanilla ice cream or fruit sherbet.

The guest rooms are simply furnished and spacious with comfortable, unpretentious décor. Most have private baths. The Nauvoo is a very popular place, and those planning a visit or a meal are advised to make reservations well in advance.

Accommodations: 14 rooms, 12 with private bath. *Pets:* Not permitted. *Driving Instructions:* Take Route 136 west from McComb, Illinois, to the Mississippi River; then go north on Route 96 to Nauvoo.

Indiana

POTAWATOMI INN

Pokagon State Park, P.O. Box 37, Angola, IN 46703. 219-833-1077. *Innkeeper:* Kenneth W. Meyers. Open all year.

Potawatomi Inn, in scenic, wooded Pokagon State Park, overlooks Lake James, the third largest natural lake in Indiana. Two years after the park was dedicated, the sprawling "old English"-style inn was built to accommodate the many people who visit the park throughout the year. The Potawatomi Inn is on an immense sweep of lawns near the widest point of the lake. An addition and a great deal of remodeling took place in 1966, when the rooms throughout were updated. The large inn is now quite modern and comfortable with an informal atmosphere. It is in the middle of an area of scenic natural beauty and many excellent recreational facilities. The inn keeps alive a trace of the park's Indian heritage by using Indian names for the guest rooms and Indian motifs in some of the public rooms. The Lonidaw Lounge is rustic, with brick walls and a patterned brick-and-concrete floor. The big brick fireplace has a fire on chilly evenings and winter days. A stuffed buffalo head peers down from the brick chimney wall above the hearth. The lounge has television and card tables, and a gift shop is nearby. The long, closed-in porch with a panoramic view of the lake provides more lounge facilities.

The Pokagon dining room seats 250 people informally for three meals each day at reasonable prices. Dinners are selected from a simple menu featuring roast beef daily and other entrées that change each day. There is usually a choice of seafood, a steak, and a chicken or ham dish with accompanying vegetables, potatoes, and dessert.

Many of the year-round facilities at the inn and the park were installed by the Civilian Conservation Corps when it was stationed here from 1934 to 1942. The men constructed gatehouses, trails, roads, several guest cabins, beaches, the bathhouse, shelters, and the saddle barn for the trail horses. They also built the 1,800-foot refrigerated toboggan slide and planted thousands of trees. The many facilities of the park are discussed in the preceding section on the Angola area.

Accommodations: 80 rooms with private bath. *Pets:* Not permitted. *Driving Instructions:* The inn and the park are 1½ miles south of the junction of the Indiana Toll Road and I-69. They are 5 miles north of Angola on Route 127.

SHERMAN HOUSE RESTAURANT AND INN

35 South Main Street, Batesville, IN 47006. 812-934-2407. *Innkeeper:* Bobbie Jean Benz. Open all year.

The Sherman House is built around one of the oldest structures in Batesville. In 1852, John Brinkman constructed the original hotel, which survives today in the present lobby, kitchen, Old Vienna Café, and Sherman Lounge. Probably named Brinkman House originally, the hotel was later renamed Sherman House in honor of William Tecumseh Sherman's feats in the Civil War. Today a number of early prints from the Sherman era form part of the décor in the lounge that bears his name. In 1923 Hillenbrand Industries, an important local business, bought the hotel and began construction of four additional buildings on the property. By 1933 these had been united into a single structure that remains today. During the construction and rebuilding of the final hotel, much of the heavy timbering, including 30-by-30 inch yellow poplar girders, was retained. In the early 1950s the hotel was thoroughly renovated and modernized. The program of modernization has continued up until recently, and the result is the mixture of décors evident today.

From the outside, the Sherman has a distinct old-world flavor with half-timbering, turned finials at the eave peaks, and small-paned leaded glass windows on the street side. Inside, the lobby has been redone in a rustic manner with exposed beams in the ceiling and wood paneling on the walls. There are several dining rooms with different décor; the Old Vienna dining room's ambience is enhanced by murals drawn by Hoosier artist Harold Hancock. Hancock also painted the armorial designs in the General Sherman Lounge and the mural in the Sherman Suite. The Sherman House offers modern air-conditioned guest rooms with television. The have twin or double beds and modern dressers and other furniture.

The Sherman House has enjoyed the reputation over many years of being one of southeastern Indiana's finer restaurants. Its location an hour's drive from either Indianapolis or Cincinnati and its proximity to Interstate 74 have meant that many highway travelers have found their way to the inn. The menu dips into the cuisine of several countries—including France, Italy, Germany—and of the

American Midwest. Appetizers range from shrimp cocktail to German sauerkraut balls to escargots Bourguignon and there are fresh soups daily. The entrée selections number twenty plus the special of the day. Fish selections include snapper from the Gulf of Mexico, lobster flown in from Maine, and flounder from the East. There are Indiana ham steak and Hoosier-style fried chicken. Enthusiasts of German food may select sauerbraten, Wiener schnitzel, or beef Stroganoff. There are frog legs for the more adventurous, and several cuts of steak for the traditional-minded.

Accommodations: 18 rooms with private bath. *Pets:* Not permitted. *Driving Instructions:* Take I-74 to Route 229 south to the inn.

Mitchell, Indiana

Mitchell is the home of *Spring Mill State Park*, named for the picturesque stone mill built in 1816 that still stands in the restored *Pioneer Village* within the park boundaries. The mill creek, dam, and flume supply the water to turn the mill's 24-foot overshot waterwheel; it, in turn, drives wooden-geared millstones, which daily grind corn into meal that may be purchased by visitors. Surrounding the mill are a number of restored buildings that have survived from the early nineteenth century. Included are the village meeting house, apothecary shop, distillery, tavern, hat shop, mill office, spring house, and barn, as well as several pioneer dwellings. A shuttle bus conducts visitors from the Pioneer Village to stops at Spring Mill Lake, a Pioneer Cemetery, and two of the park's important caverns—*Donaldson Cave* and *Twin Caves*. Boat rides are offered on the underground rivers that flow through these caves and that are famous for their population of northern blindfish. The park is also the site of the Virgil Grissom Memorial, erected in honor of the Indiana astronaut.

SPRING MILL INN

Spring Mill State Park, Mitchell, Indiana. Mailing address: P.O. Box 68, Mitchell, IN 47446. 812-849-4081. *Innkeeper:* Robert E. Chapman. Open all year.

Spring Mill Inn is one of the finest state park inns that we know. The buff-colored building, constructed in 1939 of native limestone quarried in nearby Bedford, consists of a central three-story portion with wings fanning out on either side. The inn was fully remodeled in 1976, and the result is a blending of the traditional original building with some strikingly modern additions. One is a glass-walled conference room that looks out into the treetops through an angled window wall. Another is the unusual indoor-outdoor swimming pool whose two parts are connected by a moat under a glass wall. The inn's lounge combines red wall-to-wall carpeting, wood-paneled pillars, and a large limestone fireplace with comfortable wood and plaid upholstered furniture to provide a pleasant place to read, watch television, or just enjoy the fire.

The redecorated guest rooms have quality colonial reproduction furniture, color television, and telephones. Other inn facilities include a new two-story parking garage next to the inn, tennis courts, and horseback riding stables. A game room off the pool is popular with the children of guests. The dining room at Spring Mill offers all three meals daily to both inn guests and daily visitors to the park. The standard à la carte dinner menu features the usual range of American foods. A daily special aimed to please all members of families staying at the inn might include beef stew over noodles, a complete spaghetti dinner, flounder, baked chicken, or ham and beans. The inn's special cornsticks, made from cornmeal ground at the mill in the park, are usually on the table. Hoosier hospitality and the opportunity to stay in this beautiful and historic park are two good reasons to plan a visit to Spring Mill Inn.

Accommodations: 75 rooms with private bath. *Pets:* Not permitted. *Driving Instructions:* Take Route 60 east from Mitchell to the park entrance.

New Harmony, Indiana

New Harmony is a small town in the southwest corner of the state, about a half-hour's drive from Evansville. In 1814, Father George Rapp and his followers, separatists from the Lutheran Church, settled the area. In just ten years New Harmony was being hailed as a uniquely civilized and prosperous town in the wilderness. Then, in 1825, the separatists moved back East, selling the settlement to Robert Owen, a Welsh-born Scottish industrialist and social reformer. Owen established an early utopian community there, bringing with him scientists and educators. The community soon became one of the leading intellectual centers on the emerging Midwestern frontier.

Today, buildings remain from both the settlement and the utopian periods. Visitors should drop in at the *New Harmony Visitor Center* at North and Arthur streets or call 812-682-4474 for complete information about the ambitious restoration of New Harmony and about tours of the historic sites. The sites listed below are open 9 to 5 daily except where special hours are indicated. Admission is charged for a complete tour. The complete tour includes visits to the Atheneum and Theatrum, a modern structure designed by architect Richard Meier. There are five log structures at the corner of North and West streets displaying life in the early period. The five blockhouses have been re-erected on this site. Several houses of the period are open.

THE NEW HARMONY INN

North Street, New Harmony, Indiana. Mailing address: P.O. Box 581, New Harmony, IN 47631. 812-682-4491. *Innkeeper:* Gary J. Gerard. Open all year.

There is no historic country inn in or near New Harmony, but there is a brand new inn that is most intriguing. The New Harmony Inn, completed in 1974, consists of an "entry house" that serves as the reception and registration area and a separate building with guest rooms. The New Harmony area is filled with outstanding examples of contemporary architecture that, for the most part, blend harmoniously (pun intended) with the traditional buildings going back to the early 1800s. The New Harmony is an interesting blend of traditional lines with strikingly modern interiors. The building that houses the guest rooms is a brick structure with modern single-paned windows and

several window-width balconies at the second-floor level. Many rooms have wood-burning fireplaces, and all have contemporary furnishings and décor that maintain the Indiana tradition of simplicity in line. Many have rush-seated rockers and desk chairs that, while new, reflect the heritage of Indiana furniture making. Some of the more expensive units consist of rooms with kitchenettes, living rooms, and spiral staircases that lead to sleeping "lofts." Within the entry house is a large, open-truss-roofed conference room as well as other seminar rooms that are frequently used by educational and business conferences and "retreats." A small chapel is also available to guests for meditation. The inn has a "greenhouse" swimming pool available for swimming all year. No meals are served at New Harmony Inn except breakfast, but the Red Geranium Restaurant is adjacent to the inn.

Accommodations: 45 rooms with private bath. *Pets:* Not permitted. *Driving Instructions:* New Harmony is 25 miles northwest of Evansville and is reached via Route 66, 68, or 69.

Michigan

THE TERRACE INN

216 Fairview, Bay View, MI 49770. 616-347-2410 (off season: 616-347-6280). *Innkeepers:* Sue and Charles Vorpagel. Open May through October's color season.

The Terrace Inn is on the historic grounds of the old Bay View Association, established by the Methodist Church in 1875 as part of the Chautauqua tours. The entire association grounds are on the National Register of Historic Places. Five hundred acres of land-scaped, well-maintained grounds surround the inn and many Victorian gingerbread houses. Nature trails wind through groves of oaks and maples, and hedges outline green lawns. The land rising above Little Traverse Bay has been made into terraces. The Terrace Inn is high on one of these. Dating from 1910, it was one of the last structures built by the association. A classic turn-of-the-century summer resort hostelry, the inn remains almost unchanged today except for a few modern necessities such as indoor plumbing and electricity. Its rooms are simply decorated and furnished with the original oak dressers, bedsteads, washstands, and rockers. About half have had private baths added, the others share large hall bathrooms.

The spacious lobby-parlor has a brick hearth where fires are almost always lit on chilly mornings and cool evenings after dinner. This room contains the inn's only television set. Off this room is the dining room, furnished in the original décor of utilitarian oak, including oak buffets, chairs, children's high chairs, and waitresses' sideboards. The menu features homemade soups and fresh Lake Superior whitefish, offered daily along with some three or four other entrées. Meals are served by waitresses attired in turn-of-the-century dresses and ruffled white caps, further enhancing the inn's ambience. The dining room offers full meals June through Labor Day and only complimentary breakfasts the rest of the season. No liquor is served.

On the lower terrace a Victorian ice-cream parlor stays open on warm evenings. The inn's inviting front porch, furnished with many white rockers and potted plants, is a good spot to sit and enjoy the bay breezes. A long, wide flight of red-carpeted stairs leads to the lower terrace; it is a short walk from here to the private beach and the "million dollar" sunsets over the bay. The Terrace is a venerable summer inn, peaceful and relaxing, where many guests return year after year.

Accommodations: 43 rooms, 21 with private bath. *Pets:* Not permitted. *Driving Instructions:* Bay View is at the north end of Petoskey on Route 31 and 131. Turn right at the Bay View Association entrance and follow the road to the front of the hotel.

Dearborn, Michigan

THE DEARBORN INN

20301 Oakwood Boulevard, Dearborn, MI 48123. 313-271-2700.
Innkeeper: Mr. Adrian A. de Vogel. Open all year.

The Dearborn Inn is a complex of lodgings built in 1931 by Henry Ford, with additions in 1960. Ford built the inn for the convenient accommodation of travelers who landed at the nearby Ford Airport. It was the first "airport hotel" and also served visitors to Ford's Greenfield Village and the Henry Ford Museum nearby. Accommodations are offered on the 23-acre site in three distinct life-styles: at the inn itself, in guest rooms in five reproduction colonial homes, and in two motor houses.

The inn reflects Ford's love for Georgian architecture in its imposing brick façade, which guests approach on a sweeping circular drive. The inn has a distinctly Southern feeling and appearance. Reproductions of many pieces of early American furniture are featured, as are carefully chosen wallpapers and paints that reflect the tints of the colonial period. The inn was fully air-conditioned in 1937, one of the first in the country to have this feature. With the repeal of Prohibition in the early 1930s, cocktail lounges were added to the nation's leading hotels. However, Ford was a strict teetotaler and would not permit their installation at the inn. Not until 1949, two years after his death, were a bar and cocktail lounge put into operation. The original inn offers overnight accommodations in ninety-four rooms.

In addition to rooms at the inn, visitors may choose rooms or suites in any of five colonial homes that are replicas of the homes of famous early Americans. Entrance halls, stairs, and sitting rooms are exact or close copies of the originals. The guest rooms have been slightly modified to accommodate modern conveniences such as private bathrooms. The exteriors of the homes are the same size and are made from the same materials as the originals. The Patrick Henry House, the largest of the five, was built from Virginia brick, as was the original home in Red Hill, Virginia. The furnishings of the homes are reproductions, in part, of pieces used in the original homes. The bed in which Barbara Fritchie slept, for instance, has been reproduced and stands in a bedroom in the replica of her home. The reproduction colonial houses offer a total of thirty-three rooms. There are also two motor houses for travelers who prefer facilities of this type. Fifty-four rooms are available in these accommodations.

For dining at the inn, the Early American Dining room and the pine-paneled Ten Eyck Tavern Coffee Shop offer breakfast, lunch, and dinner. A guest may start his meal with an appetizer such as Michigan bean soup. Entrées include roast prime ribs of beef and a large selection of seafood, including filet of scrod, whitefish from the Great Lakes, fresh Gulf shrimps, trout from Lake Superior, golden pickerel, and Great Lakes perch. Michigan apple pie and Dearborn Inn cheesecake head the dessert menu. On Fridays and Saturdays traditional New England "Hungry Pilgrim Dinners" are served featuring clambakes, other seafood, and a selection of steaks, chops, and roasts.

Accommodations: 180 rooms with private bath. *Driving Instructions:* The inn is on Oakwood Boulevard. Take the Oakwood Boulevard exit off either I-94 or the Southfield Freeway (M-39).

BOTSFORD INN

28000 Grand River Avenue, Farmington Hills, MI 48024. 313-474-4800. *Innkeeper:* John W. Anhut. Open all year.

In the nineteenth century, the Botsford Inn, known then as Sixteen Mile House, provided food and lodging to travelers between Detroit and Lansing on the Grand River plank road. Drovers, herdsmen, and farmers were considered the rougher element and were asked to sleep on the floor in the taproom. More refined lodgers spent the night in comparative luxury in the sleeping rooms above. After a series of owners the inn became the property of the Botsford family, who ran it from 1860 up to the time Henry Ford bought it for restoration in 1924. Ford had the place meticulously restored, supervising much of the work himself with the help of one of the Botsfords. An oral history of the inn taken at the time of restoration is in the Ford Motor Company Archives and in the library at Greenfield Village. Many rare nineteenth-century antiques and treasures went into the inn from the Ford collections and remain there today. There are original Hitchcock chairs, a buffet from General Robert E. Lee's home, and a 110-year-old Chickering piano that had belonged to General George Armstrong Custer's sister. In the front parlor is Mr. Ford's favorite, a Swiss music box, The Stella, that has perforated metal discs producing splendid sound. The inn's original rooms contain museum-quality four-poster beds, heavy-gilded mirrors, and period antique rugs, bureaus, and tables creating a nineteenth-century ambience.

In 1951, John Anhut purchased Botsford. Since then he has put on nine additions, many in keeping with the style of the original inn, and he has kept intact the period rooms, such as the old kitchen with its early utensils and décor. The suite created for Thomas Edison still has the carved white oak furnishings Ford installed for Edison when he visited the Botsford. The additions have allowed for more dining rooms, lodgings, and conference halls. Today, most of the guest rooms are furnished with good period reproductions combined with antique pieces, color television, and such other modern amenities as private bathrooms. Former stables and outbuildings have all been converted to lodging and dining facilities. Gone are the corrals that at one time held 1,000 sheep and 500 cattle on their way to market. it is just as well—all that mooing and bleating could easily disturb a sound night's sleep.

The Botsford Inn is set back from the road, thanks to Henry Ford. It is still surrounded by a white picket fence and is well landscaped. Mrs. Ford put in a walled formal garden that Mr. Anhut carefully maintains. The inn is a most popular dining experience, with easy access from Detroit. The dining rooms serve hearty early-American cuisine including such specialties as chicken pie, turkey, and trout. The Botsford, a favorite location for weddings and receptions, has rustic and more formal rooms available for buffets, banquets, and luncheons. Despite its expansion over the years, the Botsford still has appeal as a historic inn and was recently listed on the National Register of Historic Places.

Accommodations: 65 rooms with private bath. *Pets:* Restricted to the motel area. *Driving Instructions:* Take Grand River Avenue to its intersection with Eight Mile Road.

Harbor Springs, Michigan

HARBOUR INN

Beach Drive, Harbor Springs, MI 49740. 616-526-2108. *Innkeeper:* Nicholas C. Bicking. Open all year.

The Harbour Inn is an imposing turn-of-the-century resort on the shore of Little Traverse Bay off Lake Michigan. Built in 1911, the rambling white wooden structure has red rooftops at many levels on wings, additions, and porches. The resort grounds occupy about 50 acres of northern Michigan woodlands, lawn, fields, and beachfront, with vistas of the bay and lake at every turn. The large verandas are the kind meant to be furnished with wicker rockers and porch swings.

The inn's original section comprised the tower, lobby, dining area, and about thirty guest rooms. The present cocktail lounge occupies the site of an indoor putting green. In the late 1920s an enterprising young man, envisioning a large resort attracting many hundreds of guests, built a forty-room addition to the hotel and had plans to build more. What he did not envision, however, was the Crash and subsequent Great Depression. The wing was completed in the early 1930s, further work was abandoned, and the young man sold his shares. Interest in the resort was quickly renewed, and it is going strong today. The present owner, Mr. Bicking, has winterized the hotel, which now offers lodging to skiers as well as to enthusiasts of summer lakeside vacations.

The spacious lobby's oversized stone fireplace has a twin in the comfortable lounge, and fires burn in cool weather throughout the year. The lounge has comfortable groupings of soft chairs and couches around the hearth and in front of the picture windows with views of the lawns and water.

The Marine Dining Room and the Harbour Cocktail Lounge offer splendid harbor views, particularly at night when the lights of the far shores shine across the water. The dining room offers guests selections from the grill and fresh seafood. Its entrées range from traditional American hotel cuisine—such as prime ribs, stuffed flounder, and breaded veal—to fresh Lake Superior whitefish (a house specialty), Lake Michigan trout, and beef burgundy over noodles.

This full-service resort provides guests with myriad entertaining recreational and evening activities. There are tennis, horseback riding, hiking, biking, swimming in a heated outdoor pool, and boating, as well as lawn games. Skiing and golf are just minutes from the grounds. The beach is a fine place to gather driftwood and Petoskey stones, fossilized corals dating back 540 million years.

The guest rooms, including a few family suites with adjoining baths, have simple décor and hotel furnishings. Rooms are carpeted, and the walls are covered with paneling. Almost all have water views; none has television or a phone. Mr. Bicking was startled one morning by the early departure of a couple who had reserved their room for the week but were leaving after one night. They complained that sounds of the surf had kept them from sleeping and that the chirping birds had disturbed them early in the morning. Well—one man's meat is another man's poison, we've heard.

Accommodations: 65 rooms, 61 with private bath. *Driving Instructions:* The hotel is on Beach Drive, 2 miles east of Harbor Springs.

GRAND HOTEL

Mackinac Island, MI 49757. *Off-season address:* 222 Wisconsin Avenue, Lake Forest, IL 60045. Mackinac: 906-847-3331; Lake Forest: 517-332-0363. *Innkeeper:* R.D. Musser. Open mid-May to late October.

The Grand Hotel is the Dowager Queen of Mackinac Island. This beauty, though nearly a hundred years old, is vibrantly alive today, gleaming white on a bluff high above the Straits of Mackinac where Lakes Huron and Michigan touch. She stands on 500 acres of landscaped grounds with flower gardens, groves of trees, woodlands, and acres of meticulously tended lawns and hedges.

The romance of the hotel begins the moment guests arrive on the island and step into the hotel's horse-drawn carriage. The horses are decked out in plumes, and the coachman wears a top hat and hunting pinks. The carriage brings guests right to the entrance, part of the hotel's most famous feature, its porch. Said to be the longest porch in the world, it has 880 feet of columns, fluttering American flags, bright yellow awnings, and flowers everywhere. Inside, the enormous parlor is a medley of bright colors, upholstered furnishings, softly lit chandeliers, and dark carpeting. There are wallpaper murals worthy of the spacious room, and vases of seasonal flowers and after-dinner concerts complete the picture.

The resort offers guests just about every service in a luxurious setting of another era. The large formal dining room, the parlor, and the guest rooms have all been remodeled in keeping with the splendid hotel and its special setting. The waters of the Straits can be seen from many parts of the Grand. Numerous public rooms offer guests relaxation, entertainment, cocktails, light meals, and dancing. Among the services and thoughtful touches here are complimentary morning coffee, evening demitasse in the parlor, concerts accompanying afternoon teas, and many resort activities, such as horseback riding on miles of trails and horse-drawn surrey tours of the island.

Most of the hotel's rooms have picture windows offering beautiful views. Each is decorated attractively in individual styles with bold colors in fabrics and wall-coverings. Guests may chose from regular rooms, suites, deluxe bedrooms, and studio rooms. All meals are

included in the room tariff. The kitchen prides itself on the excellent Mackinac whitefish and aged prime rib of beef. The menu, which rotates every four nights, offers about ten entrées including fresh and smoked seafoods, roasts, steaks, and a number of more unusual choices that add variety and fun. There is even a nightly nonmeat dish and, of course, salads and plenty of fresh vegetables.

The hotel first opened to guests in 1887 and was run under various owners virtually without profit for much of her life. She had many ups and downs; some of the downs nearly got her razed. Eventually she become the property of the present owner's uncle, W. Stewart Woodfill, whose unflagging love and enthusiasm carried her through the Depression years and into more profitable popularity. At one time during the Depression there were 411 employees on the payroll and only eleven paying guests. The present owner, R. D. Musser, has faithfully followed in his uncle's footsteps, and the hotel is even more impresive today. it is definitely an experience, this Grand Hotel. One not to be missed.

Accommodations: 262 rooms, most with private bath. *Pets:* Not permitted. *Driving Instructions:* Ferries and airlines serve the island, which doesn't allow cars. The ferries run from Mackinaw City and from Saint Ignace on the mainland.

THE IROQUOIS

Mackinac Island, MI 49757. 906-847-3321. *Innkeepers:* Sam and Margaret McIntire. Open mid-May to mid-October.

For those who seek a first-class hotel experience while on Mackinac Island but feel overpowered by the Grand Hotel's size, the Iroquois is the perfect answer. Built as a private house at the turn of the century, it has been welcoming guests for more than seventy-five years. With time, it has grown in one direction and another but has managed to maintain the look and appeal of an earlier era. An addition completed for the 1980 summer season has resulted in an enlarged dining room and an additional twelve guest rooms and suites. Some of these are in a newly added tower and are among the most luxurious in the hotel.

For years the Iroquois has been content to be among the more expensive hotels on the island, safe in the knowledge that the standard it set would justify the price. The setting itself is worth some extra expense. The Iroquois is directly at the lakeshore, on a point of land, and the dining room and many of the guest rooms enjoy lake views. Particularly nice is dinner by candlelight, viewing the lake-freighters' far-off lights that flicker over the water. The hotel Carriage House Dining Room offers a selection of chops, steaks, prime ribs, shrimp, lobster, and country-style baked chicken. A specialty is the Lake Superior whitefish. As many as twenty desserts are offered at dinnertime. These and all breads and rolls are prepared fresh daily by the hotel's full-time pastry chef.

Throughout the Iroquois the McIntires have maintained the look of a fine home with formal wallpapers, painted white trim, wall-to-wall carpeting, and the highest quality hotel furnishings. Some guest rooms have cathedral ceilings, sitting rooms, or views from large bay windows. In warmer months guests can have cocktails outdoors overlooking the Straits of Mackinac, get a suntan on the hotel's sun deck, or sit quietly on the hotel's attractive round corner porch.

Accommodations: 47 rooms with private bath. *Pets:* Not permitted. *Driving Instructions:* Leave cars at Mackinaw City or Saint Ignace and take the ferry to the island. Alternatively, there is an air strip on the island for private airplanes.

Mackinac Island is a summer resort island that has never really bowed to the twentieth century. Although it is easy to drive to, all cars must be left behind at Mackinaw City or Saint Ignace, from which ferries convey pedestrians to the island. Compared in its feeling to the British island of Bermuda, Mackinac Island, too, relies on horse and carriage and the bicycle to provide basic transportation. It is only 9 miles around and accessible to cyclists and hikers. Mackinac Island is steeped in history. The Jesuits made it the first outpost of civilization in the Northwest. During the American Revolution, the British built a fort on the island to supplement *Fort Michilimackinac.*

THE NATIONAL HOUSE INN

102 South Parkview, Marshall, MI 49068. 616-781-7374. *Innkeepers:* Norman D. Kinney and Steven W. Poole. Open all year except Christmas Eve and Christmas Day.

Throughout the midwest there are many examples of early inns that have slowly been modernized to death. The National House is a striking exception to the trend and a perfect accompaniment to a village many call the "Williamsburg of the Midwest." Built in 1835 as a stagecoach stop, the inn has been fully restored, with modernization lmited to the installation of private bathrooms in each of the fourteen bedrooms. The inn has been listed on the national Register of Historic Places and is the oldest operating inn in the state.

Before the Civil War the inn reputedly was used as a stopping place on the Underground Railroad. The house continued its function as an inn until 1878, when it was converted to a factory that produced wagons and windmills. Just after the turn of the century, National House was converted to apartments. It remained that way until its purchase and restoration by the Kinney and Minick families. Finding the property in a sadly neglected state, the new owners set about to restore what could be restored and rebuild the remainder. In addition to installing private baths, the new innkeepers built a brick fireplace in the lobby, using bricks that had formerly blocked windows during the apartment house days. There is an additional fireplace in the upstairs lounge that bears handsome paneling and, as in the rest of the inn, a collection of early furniture. Cleverly hidden behind some of the panels are a color television set and an ice machine. The unobtrusiveness of modern conveniences at National House maintains the feeling of a century and a half of history that pervades the inn. Furnishings are varied and selected to match room by room. Thus the tone of the upstairs lounge is set by the Windsor armchairs and early rockers, while the Sidney Ketchum guest room is a Victorian masterpiece with complementing carved massive bedstead and marble-top mirrored dresser. Other guest rooms are set in the earlier period, their iron and brass beds blending with early maple or pine furniture. Throughout, the guest rooms have appropriate wallpapers that reproduce the small prints popular before the twentieth century. Downstairs is a dining

room with salmon-colored woodwork, antique oak dining tables and chairs, and a reproduction nineteenth-century folk-art hooked rug. Also on this floor is a gift shop specializing in Victorian reproduction pieces. Throughout the inn are original Currier and Ives prints selected by Mrs. Minick to complement the early furnishings. In the morning, a Continental breakfast is served, the only meal offered. In pleasant weather the Victorian sitting garden is a restful gathering place that overlooks the centerpiece of Marshall, the Brooks Memorial Fountain.

The inn contains a remarkable assemblage of early and Victorian-era Americana. It was at one time a popular stagecoach stop on the run between Detroit and Chicago. Today, its proximity to I-94, the twentieth-century equivalent connecting the two great cities, means that the modern traveler can enjoy the same convenience in surroundings that are a good deal more comfortable than they were a century and a half ago.

Accommodations: 14 rooms with private bath (2 share shower only). *Pets:* Not permitted. *Driving Instructions:* From I-94, use exit 110 and follow old Route 27 south 1½ miles to the inn. From I-69, exit at Michigan Avenue in Marshall and go straight 1½ miles to the inn.

Saint Clair, Michigan

ST. CLAIR INN

    500 North Riverside, Saint Clair, MI 48079. 313-329-2222. *Innkeeper:* Mike LaPorte. Open all year.

The St. Clair Inn is in many respects a country inn grown up. The Tudor-style inn was built in 1926, and a number of additions were made in the years that followed. Today, the two-story brick riverfront building and its companion houses offer lodging in seventy rooms and suites and dining in six dining rooms. As you enter the St. Clair and step onto the cobblestone floor of the entrance hall, you look ahead through the windows of the large lobby to a view—of the river and the Canadian shore beyond—that is repeated in the dining rooms and many of the guest rooms. The lobby sets the scene for the rooms that follow with its beige rough-plaster walls, two fireplaces, forest-green ceiling, and beams supported by four oak pillars.

The dining rooms vary in size and décor. You may eat in the grand English dining room with its large beams and contrasting smaller beams, banks of large, multipaned windows, ivy-patterned linen, and leaded-glass doors leading to the porch dining rooms. A smaller Garden Dining Room has crystal chandeliers with Austrian shades, an antique mirror, and Victorian chairs and wallpaper. Somewhat less formal are the north and south dining rooms, with barn-board ceilings and heavy exposed beams. The Veranda Dining Room has picture windows that run to the ceiling, which is a continuation of the barn-board and beamed ceiling that prevails in many of the public rooms. On the walls are photographs of some of the freighters that have formed the backbone of lake commerce for so many years. The Coach Room has a piano bar and a fireplace and is decorated with stained glass.

The menu used in the six dining rooms is extensive as befits a place of this size. The many seafood selections reflect the inn's proximity to Lake Huron and include northern Canadian walleye shark, scrod, shrimps, scallops, frogs' legs, and king crab. In addition, there are steak, prime ribs, chicken Kiev, and pork chops, a house specialty. The St. Clair has employed the same pastry chef for more than thirty years, and among the dessert specialties is a fresh strawberry pie brimming with whole fresh strawberries.

Fifty of the guest rooms are in the main inn, where accommodations vary from room to room. Two, for example, have Hitchcock-style furniture and arch-topped French doors that open onto a private deck. A third room has a brass bed, and still others are furnished with hotel-style furniture dating back to the period when the hotel was built. There are also seven connecting pine-paneled cottages that face the river, a three-bedroom Captain's House with a sunken living room, a fireplace, and nautical décor, and ten Annex rooms that open onto an outside deck. Eight one- or two-bedroom apartments called the River Station Suites are available for a nightly rental.

Accommodations: 70 rooms and suites, all with private bath. *Pets:* Not permitted. *Driving Instructions:* The inn is a few miles east of I-94 on the bank of the Saint Clair River in downtown Saint Clair.

Minnesota

Grand Marais, Minnesota

CASCADE LODGE

Route 61, Grand Marais, MN 55640. 218-387-1112. *Innkeepers:* Carl and Mae Odmark. Open all year.

Cascade Lodge, a clapboard-over-log and stone building, is separated only by Route 61 from the rockbound coast of Lake Superior. Built in 1930, the lodge has grown and been modernized over the years but has consistently resisted the chrome and plastic look that befell many of its competitors. The 1980s Cascade Lodge consists of the main building with its guest rooms, a detached restaurant in a similar architectural style, and a dozen guest cabins. Behind the buildings stretches a seemingly endless aspen forest laced with hiking trails that become cross-country skiing trails at the first snowfall.

The Odmarks have maintained the feeling of home throughout the lodge and cabins. Rooms are varied; those in the lodge have plaster walls, carpeting, and hot-water heating. Some of the cabins are built of logs and retain their natural log-wall interiors, while others have painted or paneled walls. Each guest room, regardless of location, has its own modern bathroom with both shower and tub.

The Fireplace Room at the lodge is dominated by its radial-beam ceiling culminating in an authentic wagon-wheel light fixture with copper candle lights. There are also a natural-stone fireplace with a copper canopy, a picture window overlooking Lake Superior, and comfortable furnishings that invite guests to linger and relax. Opening off this room through a triple door is another room with a picture window facing the lake, a grand piano, television, a game table, desks, and comfortable sofas and chairs. A large collection of trophy animal mounts and skins including those of timber wolves, moose, bear, coyote, geese, and fish decorate the lounges and the dining room.

The restaurant, also overlooking the lake, has a trussed ceiling with exposed heavy beams, wagon-wheel and hurricane-lamp chandeliers, and a stone fireplace at one end. The restaurant's large menu offers about fifteen fish and seafood offerings and an equal number of meat and poultry dishes. Dinner entrées include several steak and seafood combination plates as well as a number of omelets, such as cheese or Spanish. House specialties include Lake Superior trout, barbecued ribs, and charcoal-broiled steaks. Many guests ask especially for the barbecued chicken wings offered as an appetizer, or for their whole "deep browned" potatoes made according to a secret recipe.

In winter the focus of activity at the lodge is its excellent 33-mile cross-country ski trail system, which the Odmarks regularly have groomed. Snowshoeing is also popular, and photographers often capture the antics of the semi-tame deer that come to the lodge to eat food set out for them. In summer, Cascade Creek flows between the cabins to the lake; several hiking trails wind back between the creek and the river to Lookout Mountain. The Cascade Creek Nature Trail has been laid out with thirty-one numbered stopping places so guests can inspect firsthand the flora and fauna of the surrounding woodland. The lodge will be happy to furnish a guide for those who want to find the best local fishing spots. Families traveling with children will be pleased with the number of planned games, crafts, and other activities at the lodge.

Accommodations: 13 rooms and 12 cabins, all with private bath. *Pets:* Permitted in cabins only. *Driving Instructions:* The lodge is 9 miles southwest of Grand Marais on Route 61.

GUNFLINT LODGE

Gunflint Trail, Grand Marais, Minnesota. *Mailing address:* P.O. Box 100 G.T., Grand Marais, MN 55604. 218-388-2294. *Innkeepers:* Bruce and Sue Kerfoot. Open May 15 to October 15.

Gunflint Lake, at an elevation of 1,543 feet, lies along the Canadian border 43 miles inland from the Lake Superior shore at Grand Marais. Here, the Kerfoot family has been welcoming guests to their lodge for more than 50 years. First opened in 1928, the lodge complex has grown almost every year. There are now eight cabins, four suites in the Trading Post building, two chalets, a sauna, and the main lodge. Fully developed family recreational activities include a children's playground, badminton, shuffleboard, tennis, and a marina offering sailing, water skiing, pontoon boats, and a swimming raft. The surrounding woods have a network of hiking trails. The Gunflint Northwoods Outfitters, with headquarters on the property, organized canoe trips throughout the surrounding million-acre Boundary Waters Wilderness Area.

Accommodations vary in architectural style from rustic log cabins to frame clapboard buildings to modern A-frame chalets. Most have fireplaces and are pine-paneled. Cabins range in size from one to four bedrooms and are furnished with linen and towels. Furniture tends to be modern in the guest cabins, most of which have supplementary electric heat.

Gunflint's main lodge is a rustic building with a trussed roof having exposed heavy beams; it has polished hardwood floors with braided area rugs and upholstered casual redwood furniture. One wall consists of a native-stone fireplace and large picture windows overlooking the lake and the Canadian shore in the distance. Another wall is a library corner filled with books; still another has card tables where guests often gather for bridge. Next to the lounge is the dining room, where back-country log chairs are drawn up to pine tables. Here, too, a fire burns on cool days.

The lodge serves a variety of home-cooked meals. Typical breakfasts include fresh fruit juice (a luxury this far from city life), cereals, pancakes, eggs, French toast, and bacon or sausage. The choice at lunch is usually between a hot dish like chicken à la king and a cold plate or sandwiches. The lodge will pack picnic lunches for guests who want to spend the day on the lake. Typical dinner entrées are baked chicken, fried shrimp, or roast pork. On most summer Sundays the lodge has a lavish smorgasbord that attracts diners from miles around. Monday evenings traditionally offer spaghetti and pizza dinners, and there is often a midweek outdoor barbecue.

One of the special features of Gunflint Lodge is its strong naturalist program. Each week the several resident staff members lead activities from a list of more than thirty, including outings to study a beaver colony, a magnetic rock trip, and a wildflower identification trip. Indoor activities include candlemaking, rock tumbling, and wreath making. Because of this, the lodge has become particularly popular with families traveling together. Children frequently remain in camp while the parents enjoy north-country fishing for walleye, lake trout, bass, or northern.

Accommodations: 14 rooms or suites in cabins or chalets, all with private bath. *Driving Instructions:* Take U.S. 61 to Grand Marais; then head inland for 44 miles along the Gunflint Trail (Route 12) to the lodge.

New Prague, Minnesota

SCHUMACHER'S NEW PRAGUE HOTEL

212 West Main Street, New Prague, MN 56071. 612-758-2133 (Metro: 612-445-7285). *Innkeepers:* John and Nancy Schumacher. Open all year except December 24 to 26.

When John and Nancy Schumacher first discovered New Prague in 1974, they fell in love with both the Czechoslovakian and German town and its small hotel. Built in 1898 to a design by Cass Gilbert, the architect of the Minnesota state capitol, the hotel desperately needed a complete renovation. But the Schumachers realized that here was the framework with which to realize their dream of creating a romantic country inn serving superb food. Their dream has come true. The hotel goes well past being just a fine restoration; it is designed to evoke memories of tiny Bavarian or Austrian inns by means of Nancy's decorative touches.

This inn clearly set out to cater to sentimentalists of all ages. It has flowery canopied beds, quilted comforters and down pillows you can sink back into, and even a semicircular bed with a mirrored semicircular headboard. There are antique chests with painted panels, claw-foot tubs with flowered sides, private guest room corners with pierced-heart-back chairs. Each room is named for a month of the year, the name proclaimed on unusual painted medallions above each door. Imported from Munich, the "Oktober" medallion, for example, shows a Bavarian farmer sowing his fields. The deep mulberry color of the room is highlighted with hand-painted pink chrysanthemums. Imported Bavarian lamps, an Austrian tablecloth, Persian rugs, and tapestry hangings combine with a dark, antique-finished double bed to carry out the hotel's European theme. In the "Mai" room, the canopy bed is so high that a small ladder has been installed to provide easy access. The storybook design over the bed pictures life from newlywed to old age. The "August" room has a primitive red-heart stencil design on the floors, a theme that extends to chairs and table. The rooms for every month are captivating in spirit and décor.

Because the hotel is a comfortable drive from the metropolian area, many guests come out specifically to sample the very special cuisine. The hotel's executive chef, John has researched his extensive menu with care and created more than thirty dishes, which reflect the town's Czech and German traditions, a distinctly French influence, and a touch of regional Minnesota. John's specialties are his quail stuffed with plums, pheasant in cream with mushrooms and shallots, roast duck the Czech way with caraway seeds, and several types of schnitzel. Dishes frequently come with dumplings, red cabbage, sauerkraut, or spatzle. Each is individually prepared, and there are full-course feasts for one or two as well as numerous à la carte offerings. Each of the three dining rooms has a different feeling. The largest has a large collection of Bavarian crystal, and a smaller one has a collection of Bavarian folk art.

A recent addition at the hotel is Big Cally's Bar, named for John's father, Carlton Schumacher. Nancy commissioned custom-crafted leaded windows and cabinets that incorporated hand-painted glass imported from Germany. One can sit at the antique marble bar on unusual wooden stools with handcarved "boot" feet designed by Nancy. Czech and German beers and a variety of cocktails are served in this room, which is presided over by a carved wooden Bavarian friar, imported from Germany. This room is just one more reason to go out of your way to stay in New Prague.

Accommodations: 12 rooms with private bath. *Pets and Children:* Pets are not permitted, and children are not encouraged. *Driving Instructions:* From Minneapolis, take Route 35W South to Route 13 South. Go through Savage and Prior Lake, staying on Route 13 into New Prague (about 35 miles from the metropolitan area).

New Prague is a small farming community enriched by its large Czechoslovakian and German populations. Nearby are an eighteen-hole golf course, tennis courts at local parks, and cross-country skiing on the Minnesota Valley Ski Trail. Fishing is available at Cedar lake; the Minnesota River just 9 miles away is a popular canoeing spot.

Sauk Centre, Minnesota

PALMER HOUSE HOTEL AND RESTAURANT
500 Sinclair Lewis Avenue, Sauk Centre, MN 56378. 612-352-3431.
Innkeepers: R. J. Schwartz and Al Tingley. Open all year.

For many years, the old Sauk Centre House stood on a corner of
Main Street. Although the building was serviceable, most of the local
residents felt that it had outlived its usefulness, and they longed for a
really first-class hotel. Then, in 1900, it burned to the ground, paving
the way for the construction of the Palmer House by Richard L.
Palmer two years later. The resulting three-story brick hotel with
curved-arch, stained-glass windows on the street level satisfied the
townspeople and served the community well for the next quarter
century or so.

One later-to-be-distinguished employee in this heyday period at
the Palmer House was Sinclair Lewis. While in high school he worked
at the hotel for spending money. But his personal distinction did not,
apparently, include an aptitude for hotel work. He was an exaspera-
tion to the management and was finally fired for daydreaming. The

story goes that Lewis was given specific instructions by a traveling salesman to awaken him at 2:30 A.M. so that he could catch a train. Young Mr. Lewis became so engrossed in reading that he lost track of time. At 3:00 A.M. he realized that he had forgotten the wake-up call and went to remind the gentleman of the time. Later Lewis would use his experiences at the Palmer House as a basis for his novel *Work of Art*.

By the mid-1920s the railroad began to be supplanted by the automobile as the main means of transportation, and business at Palmer House dwindled. By the time Al Tingley and Richard Schwartz discovered the place, it was sadly in need of repairs.

Friends since college days, the current owners bought the hotel in 1974, using some of the profits realized from an earlier restoration of a mansion in Saint Paul. At first, the project almost overwhelmed them, because they had to replace part of the roof, redo the plumbing and electrical systems, and then proceed from room to room to restore the hotel to its original state. Although the hotel has many handsome features, it never was regarded as having Victorian elegance. Instead, it had been designed to provide comfort to the legions of "drummers" (traveling salesmen) who passed through with their sample cases bulging with goods to be sold to the local merchants. When the new owners took over, the original features from the traveling-salesman era survived intact but had been hidden. The original tin ceiling in the lobby and the curved stained-glass windows had only to be re-exposed.

Many of the hotel's restored guest rooms have such original furnishings as the writing desks, chairs and beds. Floral prints on the walls, electrified wall sconces, and chenille bedspreads hark back to the earlier period. Rooms without a bath have a wall sink, a step up from the even earlier bowl and pitcher of cold water.

The Palmer House Restaurant serves three meals a day to guests and the public. The restaurant serves typically Midwestern "home cooking" that features steaks, roast beef and pork, fried ham, country-style ribs, baked or fried chicken and dressing, and chicken Pauline (baked in a wine sauce). Specials often include Cornish game hen, Hawaiian chicken, beef in burgundy, and shishkabob.

Accommodations: 37 rooms, 4 with private bath. *Driving Instructions:* Sauk Centre is halfway between the twin cities and Fargo, North Dakota, on I-94 and Highway 71.

Stillwater, Minnesota

LOWELL INN

102 North Second Street, Stillwater, MN 55082. 612-439-1100.
Innkeepers: Arthur and Maureen Palmer. Open all year.

The Lowell Inn, an imposing brick hotel, stands on the corner formerly occupied by the Sawyer House, which was built in 1848 and succumbed to the wrecker's ball in 1924. Completed six years later, the Lowell opened its doors on Christmas Day to serve its first meal. The inn was the dream of Nelle and Arthur Palmer, Sr. Both had spent much of their youth on the road—she as an actress and he as a pianist. Their traveling life showed them how often hostelries missed the mark and gave them an ambition to do the job right. They did not actually own the inn but served as managers for the owner, Elmore Lowell. The Palmers set out to fill the inn with a collection of fine antiques, augmented by the best linens, furniture, and other accoutrements of the hotel trade they could find. In 1945 the Palmers finally realized their lifelong dream and purchased the inn. In time they were joined by their children in the innkeeping business, as the Lowell continued to prosper. Arthur, Sr., died in 1951 and Nelle in 1970, but the tradition of excellence established by the parents is carried on by Arthur, Jr., and Maureen.

The inn comprises guest rooms and several dining rooms housed in a Williamsburg-style brick building dominated on the street side by a full-length veranda, the roof of which is supported by thirteen two-story columns. Each column represents one of the gable ends of the long roof. Four small dormer windows jut from the fourth-floor roof and overlook the balcony surrounding the veranda roof at the third-floor level.

Within the inn are three dining rooms, each quite different from the others. The George Washington, the first of the dining rooms, was opened by Nelle Palmer in 1930. It has Capo di Monte porcelains, Sheffield silver services, and a Dresden china collection displayed on the sideboards about the room. Ladderback chairs in the Williamsburg style and portraits of George and Martha Washington help set the colonial style. In 1939, Arthur, Sr., decided to build a second dining room with an outdoor trout pool from which guests could select their own trout dinner. When the natural springs in the adjoining hillside began to seep into the new room, Arthur decided to move the pool indoors and make it a centerpiece of the décor. The menu served in these two dining rooms varies somewhat from weekdays to Sundays but generally includes broiled chicken with country gravy, lamb chops, chicken livers with morelles sauce, fresh brook trout, fillet of pike, filet mignon, sirloin steak, fried shrimp, and several other selections. The dinner menu has received acclaim from the day the restaurant opened. Its most recent accolade was the award of four stars for both dining and hotel accomodations by the *Mobil Guide*.

The lobby and the guest rooms on the two upper floors reflect the love of Nelle and Arthur, Sr., for the French provincial, combined with the mood of Williamsburg. Some rooms have been recently redecorated with hand-carved Mexican sinks, whirlpool baths, thick carpeting, and overstuffed sofas. Most of the others retain the colonial antiques and complementing decorations established by the Palmers over many years.

Accommodations: 20 rooms with private bath. *Pets:* Not permitted. *Driving Instructions:* From Saint Paul take Route 36 east. Route 36 becomes Main Street in Stillwater. Turn left at the second light onto Myrtle and go one block to Second Street. Turn right, and the inn is on the corner.

Wabasha, Minnesota

THE ANDERSON HOUSE

333 Main Street, Wabasha, MN 55981. 612-565-4524. *Innkeepers:* Jeanne, John, and Gayla Hall. Open every day of the year except Christmas.

If one were to ask a fancier of country inns what he or she looked for in an inn, the list would probably include warm, congenial, experienced innkeepers; a quiet setting, perhaps overlooking a river; original antique furnishings in a historic building; a friendly house cat or two; some hot bricks to warm chilly sheets in a quilt-covered bed; and lots of good country cooking with perhaps more than one or two kinds of fragrant home-baked breads.

Such a connoisseur certainly will not be disappointed at the Anderson House in Wabasha, Minnesota, which meets all the above requirements and offers much more. As Minnesota's oldest operating hotel, it is in the National Registry of Historic Places. It has been in continuous service to hungry and weary travelers since its opening in 1856 and has been in the same family for four—"going on five"—generations. In 1901, Grandma Ida Hoffman Anderson purchased and ran the Anderson House. Ann McCaffrey, of the third generation to run the hotel, has presided over the pastry department for more than thirty years. John Shields Hall, Ida's great-grandson, and his Norwegian wife, Gayla, now run the hotel with John's mother, Jeanne Hall. Time seems to have stood still here; everything is just as Grandma would have wanted it. The timelessness of the inn is more than a mere coincidence: Most of the antique clocks in the rooms either have stopped or insist on telling different times.

The brick hotel overlooks the Mississippi River in the residential section of Wabasha, which has large yards, gardens, and flowers everywhere. Every room has antiques and Victorian furnishings, many of museum quality, from the hotel's early beginnings. Beyond the entry hall is a spacious lobby, where Ida's Old Fashioned Ice Cream Parlor has been installed in one corner of the huge room. The parlor offers, besides meals, fountain concoctions in a bright room decorated with red-and-white wallpapers, white bentwood chairs, and magazine covers dating back to the mid-nineteenth century. Green plants are tucked everywhere throughout the hotel. The Writing Room off the lobby, which has been converted to an antique shop, sells antique glassware as well as local arts and crafts. It is run by Johanna Hall, with the apparent moral support of a myna bird named Jimmy. A bevy of cats make up the rest of the Anderson House menagerie. While guests pamper the cats, they themselves are pampered by the Halls and their staff. There are hot bricks to warm the beds and mustard plasters if one feels a chill coming on; dusty shoes left outside the bedroom door at night return bright and shiny the next morning.

The Anderson House's guest bedrooms include a few in housekeeping cottages in back of the hotel. Each room has a different wallpaper, and hand-made quilts pick up the colors of the walls. The quilts are either antique or hand-sewn by two ladies in the Wabasha Nursing Home. The beds, bureaus, and nightstands are curly maple, dark mahogany, and rich walnut. There are elaborate settees, cushioned Victorian chairs, and marble-top dressers in rooms looking out over the Mississippi and the inn's gardens. Many rooms have private baths, and the remainder share old-fashioned hall bathrooms.

Downstairs, guests will find some of the best Pennsylvania Dutch cooking outside of Lancaster County, Pennsylvania. Although not all the cooking is "plain peoples' food," it certainly is the main attraction. Grandma Ida Anderson learned her cooking skills at her mother's side in Pennsylvania before coming to Minnesota. The rest of the family has learned from her, and the results show it. The Halls maintain a nearby family farm, which supplies the kitchen with fruits, vegetables, eggs, and nuts. For breakfast, guests are offered cinnamon rolls and hot sticky buns, home-cured ham, cornmeal mush, red flannel hash, eggs, scrapple, and donuts. Other meals are no less impressive. Favorite soups are Pennsylvania Dutch chicken-corn chowder, bacon corn chowder, Dutch beer and cheese soup, and a chicken soup with homemade noodles. Entrées include chicken with Dutch dumplings, deep-dish chicken pies with butter crusts, smoked stuffed pork chops served with a special braised red cabbage, pork tenderloin medallions cooked in sauerkraut, and much more. The breads include such temptations as Kugelhopf, blueberry Streusel, and Swedish limpa. The desserts are well worth an attempt to save a little room, if possible: shoo-fly pie, brown-brittle peanut pie, lemon cloud pie, sour cream raisin pie, and White House coconut torte. The list goes on and on. Anderson House serves no hard liquor but has a selection of wines and beers in the "Lost Dutchman" Bar. This inn provides a truly memorable experience in a "turn of the century" country setting.

Accommodations: 51 rooms, 35 with private bath. *Pets:* Permitted in some areas—inquire beforehand. *Driving Instructions:* Minnesota Route 61 and Route 60 go through the town of Wabasha. The inn is on the main street.

Ohio

THE BUXTON INN
   313 East Broadway, Granville, OH 43023. 614-587-0001. *Innkeepers:* Orville and Audrey Orr. Open all year.

The Buxton Inn has been in continuous operation since it was built in 1812 by Samuel Thrall as the third tavern in the newly settled village. For many years the inn served as the Granville Post Office and a popular stop on the stagecoach line from Newark, Ohio, to Columbus. In the basement, one can still see the large fireplace where the early stage drivers cooked their meals and slept under hand-hewn beams on beds of straw. In 1852 a two-story wing was added to the original building so that the structure formed a U shape with a central courtyard. The property was purchased in 1865 by Major Buxton of Alexandria, and he and his wife operated it as a hotel for forty years, until his death in 1905. The current innkeepers purchased the place in 1972 and spent two years researching and restoring it.

   Today, the Buxton Inn is almost as it was a hundred or more years ago. Perhaps one of its most unusual features is that it was constructed almost entirely of black walnut, including much of the frame, the siding, and the pillars. The exterior is painted a peach color

selected to reflect its New England heritage. The front portion is the oldest and now contains the gift shop, lobby, and main dining room on the first floor and a two-bedroom suite and two private dining rooms on the second. The 1852 addition to the rear of the inn contains the Victorian dining room on the first floor and two guest rooms on the second. Also upstairs is the original ballroom of the early tavern. It is used for receptions, special parties, and as an accessory dining room on weekends.

The Buxton Inn serves a Continental breakfast to its guests and has full luncheon and dinner menus for guests and the public alike. Several seafood selections include fresh Boston scrod sautéed with lemon butter, brook trout stuffed with mushroom dressing, fillet of sole Veronique, shrimp Italienne, coquille of seafood cardinale, and a fresh fish of the day. Other choices at dinner include quiche, chicken, sautéed beef liver with tangy orange sauce, several kinds of steak, and prime ribs. In addition to the regular soups, which include Buxton navy bean and French onion, there are special soups of the day. Two particular favorites are black mushrooms with whipped cream and cream of chicken curry with green grapes and toasted almonds. There is a wide selection of rich desserts and a rather large wine list.

If you are planning to spent the night at the Buxton Inn, it is important to make reservations early because there are only three guest rooms. One is a two-bedroom suite with Eastlake Victorian furnishings that blend with the Oriental rugs that cover the hand-pegged walnut plank floors. The first of the upstairs bedrooms in the 1852 wing is done in Empire furnishings that include a large sleigh bed. The other is actually a mini-suite with a very small room with a double bed and a larger room with an assortment of Victorian furniture including a high-backed carved bed and marble-top dressers.

The entire inn is centrally air-conditioned in the summer, and there are fireplaces in the lobby and the main dining room for extra comfort in the winter. The Buxton Inn has been placed on the National Register of Historic Places.

Accommodations: 3 rooms with private bath. *Pets:* Not permitted. *Driving Instructions:* From Columbus take Route 70 to Route 37 and drive north. Granville is 9 miles north of I-70.

THE GRANVILLE INN

314 East Broadway, Granville, OH 43023. 614-587-3333. *Innkeeper:* Jennifer Utrevis. Open all year.

The Granville Inn began as the Granville Female College in 1838; in 1861, a two-story brick lodging was added to house more students. The newer brick section remained part of the new Granville Inn after coal magnate John Sutphin Jones had torn down the wooden portion of the college and constructed a handsome model of an English country house on the land in 1924. The inn, designed for Jones by architect Frank Packard, was built of native sandstone quarried from Jones's nearby country estate, Bryn Du Farm. The finest woods and other materials went into its construction, and no expense was spared. In the mid-1970s, Paul and Robert Kent, a father and son from Granville, purchased the inn at a sheriff's sale and spent more than three years totally renovating it.

The inn is on the main street of this little New England-like town on Raccoon Creek. The lawn in front of the inn has tall trees and landscaped gardens. Drinks are served on the stone patio here, where guests can watch the activities of the town.

Inside the entrance hall and lobby the Kents have meticulously restored the wood paneling of the walls to bring up their warm hues. The polished wood floors are covered with Oriental rugs. Flanking the large stone fireplace are high-backed Windsor chairs, and a large

window seat is in the alcove in front of the tall bay window. There are thirty-three guest rooms down the wood-paneled halls. Each has been completely refurbished with new carpets, mattresses, air conditioning, and restored old-English furnishings. Each of these rooms has a special personality because of its individual flowered wallpaper, drapes, counterpanes, and furniture of dark, heavy wood.

Downstairs, guests will find a dining room and an English pub lit by the glow of candles and fires in large stone fireplaces. Waitresses dressed in long burgundy skirts with blouses and white aprons serve lunches and dinners to both guests and the public. Continental breakfasts are also provided for guests at the inn. People come from all over just to sample the famous home-baked raisin breads served with honey buter and the walnut pies and cakes served warm from the oven at all meals. Dinners begin with a choice of the inn's special hors d'oeuvres. A favorite is "Angels on horseback," from an authentic old English recipe, which consists of fresh oysters wrapped in bacon and baked in lemon butter. The entrées include a variety of steaks and roasts and the house specialties—roast duckling with burgundy sauce, and steak and quail with herbs. Entrées are accompanied by fresh salads and vegetables, the raisin bread, and hot coffee or tea.

Accommodations: 33 rooms with private bath. *Pets:* Not permitted. *Driving Instructions:* From I-70 to the east of Columbus, take Route 37 north to Granville. From Columbus, Route 161 or Route 16 goes east direct to Granville.

THE GOLDEN LAMB

27 South Broadway, Lebanon, OH 45036. 513-932-5065. *Innkeeper:* Jackson Reynolds. Open daily except Christmas.

The Golden Lamb, a large four-story street-front hotel, has been offering overnight accommodations to travelers ever since Jonas Seaman was issued a license to operate a "house of public entertainment" in 1803. Additions to the building occurred in the decades immediately following, and today the inn offers guests a choice of seventeen guest rooms as well as nine dining rooms. The lobby of the hotel sets the stage for the inn as a whole. Many early Ohio antique pieces grace the room, including a fine Regina music box that still plays the old steel-disc records. The lobby has a working fireplace, and the four first-floor dining rooms are entered from the lobby. The dining rooms are filled with antiques, as are many of the hallways throughout the inn. The Shaker Dining Room, for example, has walls lined with pegs on which hang numerous Shaker items, most of which are used daily. The inn prides itself on its collection of Shaker furniture and accessories, largely from the immediate area. In addition to the Shaker collection, the inn displays a large number of Currier and Ives prints on the walls. Guests and day visitors who wish to see more of the inn's Shaker collection are directed to the fourth floor, where three rooms have been established as museum rooms and are glassed in to allow viewing only. In addition to the lobby and dining rooms on the first floor, the Black Horse Tavern, just off the Lebanon Dining Room near the rear of the building, is maintained in mid-nineteenth century style with a long bar. The walls are decorated with old flintlock rifles and numerous horse-racing items. Horse racing was then and is today an important part of the life in Lebanon.

Each guest room is decorated in a different manner, using Shaker and other antique furniture where possible. The Charles Dickens Room (named for a guest at the inn in 1842) has a replica of the Lincoln bed as its centerpiece. Along with the high-back carved bed are a marble-top dresser with mirror and several Victorian chairs. The bathroom, like the others in the inn, is of more modern construction. The Governor DeWitt Clinton Room, named after the former Governor of New York, has a canopied four-poster, wingback chairs, an

antique secretary, and a view out over the balcony to Main Street below. The balcony, a dominant part of the building façade, is a three-story construction but is not accessible from the guest rooms.

The inn features several selections daily at dinner. Turkey in various forms has become one of the favorites. The inn serves fresh turkey raised especially for its kitchen by a local farm. Other menu regulars include roast duck with giblet or orange gravy and a lamb selection, such as roast leg or lamb shanks. There are also daily steak selections. The inn imports fresh trout once a week by direct air flight from Colorado. A regional favorite is the pan-fried Kentucky (salt-cured) ham steak served with a bourbon glaze. Among the numerous dessert selections are the popular Sister Liazie's Shaker Sugar Pie, Harvey Wallbanger cake, and a pecan pie that uses the recipe developed by Abigail Adams.

Accommodations: 17 rooms, 16 with private bath. *Pets:* Not permitted. *Driving Instructions:* The inn is in the center of Lebanon, which is most easily reached by taking Route 63 east from I-75 or Route 123 northwest from I-71.

Wisconsin

GREUNKE'S INN

17 Rittenhouse Avenue, Bayfield, WI 54814. 715-779-5480. *Innkeeper:* Judith Lokken-Strom. Open April to mid-January.

Stepping into Greunke's Inn is much like stepping into one of Norman Rockwell's *Saturday Evening Post* illustrations. Little has changed here since the late 1940s. The ice cream parlor walls display 1945 Coca-Cola calendars and trays. An old stuffed fish, snagged long ago, guards the archway to the washrooms with their glossy dark-green paint. Guests relax in the lobby to the soulful strains of Hank Williams's "Your Cheatin' Heart" and Rosemary Clooney's "Hey There" played on the old Wurlitzer juke box with its tubes of bright colors. In one corner a potbelly stove adds warmth. This is a gathering spot for lodgers, the scene of many late-night get-togethers.

The inn stands amid birches and maples at one of Bayfield's central intersections. The red wood-frame building with black shutters, built in the 1870s, could easily blend into the main street of any one of Rockwell's New England towns. The innkeeper, Judith Lokken-Strom, has carefully maintained the inn's uncomplicated atmosphere and a look that has remained untouched since the days of ownership by the Greunke family in the late 1940s and the early 1950s.

A small dining room is decorated with 1940s prints, drawings, and

antiques. It opens for business at 5 A.M. for local fishermen. Judith preserves all kinds of berries and fruits and bakes homemade pies, cakes, and pastries. House specialties are the poached whitefish and an unusual dish, whitefish livers. There are wild blueberry pancakes and pancakes topped with strawberries and whipped cream. The homemade pea soup is a daily favorite.

The warmth of the inn extends upstairs to the guest rooms, which are completely furnished with antiques of the bygone era. At the top of the stairs is an old working Swedish wall phone that guests love. A small second-floor porch on the east side of the hotel offers guests views of Lake Superior.

Accommodations: 6 rooms sharing hall baths. *Driving Instructions:* Bayfield is on Route 13, at the very top of the state, 70 miles east of Duluth.

THE MANSION

7 Rice Avenue, Bayfield, Wisconsin. *Mailing address:* P.O. Box
393, Bayfield, WI 54814. 715-779-5408. *Mansionkeeper:* Paul
Turner. Open all year.

This is not a country inn, but it is quite an experience. The Mansion, a
large Victorian estate, was built at the turn of the century as a private
home. It is still a private home, now belonging to Paul Turner, who
takes great pleasure in sharing, with one couple at a time, this grand
old structure listed on the National Register of Historic Places. He is
not an innkeeper but rather the gracious host.

The Mansion overlooks Lake Superior and the Apostle Islands
National Lakeshore. The guest bedroom, the Cathedral Room, has a
spacious balcony with outstanding vistas. The entire house is
museum-like in its period décor. The guest room's working fireplace
is kept well stocked with firewood. The room's centerpiece is a
Renaissance-style bedstead rising 8½ feet above the floor and part of
an ornate, one-of-a-kind bedroom set. A dinner for two may be
served here in front of the fireplace, in the formal dining room if
guests prefer, or out on the private balcony. The Mansion contains
music rooms, parlors, a game room, and more, which are open for a

public tour at 11 A.M. and 4 P.M. almost every day. Continental breakfasts are served at guests' whim.

Many special treats are in store at the Mansion. Mr. Turner plays the pipe organ and piano and will, if requested, play for guests. They are also treated to tours of the Mansion and special sightseeing trips in the imposing limousine. If the visiting couple would like the company of one or two personal friends, an adjoining guest bedroom—the Gold Room—is available to them.

The mansion—obviously not everyone's cup of tea, as guests have a great deal of personal attention and service devoted to them—is quite an attraction and an unusual experience.

Accommodations: 2 rooms with bath. *Pets and Children:* Occasionally permitted. *Driving Instructions:* The Mansion is 26 miles north of Ashland on Route 13.

OLD RITTENHOUSE INN

301 Rittenhouse Avenue, Bayfield, WI 54814. 715-779-5765. *Innkeepers:* Jerald J. and Mary M. Phillips. Open all year except November.

The Old Rittenhouse Inn is an 1890s mansard-roofed Victorian mansion with a brick first floor and red shake shingles on the top three floors. The structure is surrounded by a wide veranda. As you enter the inn you are greeted by the original foyer of the home, which retains its early chair-rail-height cherry paneling. The staircase, also in cherry, is on the right, and three dining rooms are on the left. As you enter the dining rooms, you are struck by the variety of Victorian lighting fixtures that have been restored and are in use there and throughout the inn. Mary and Jerry Phillips were collectors of period lighting devices before they became innkeepers. They quip that they were forced to buy the inn just to have a place to use all their lamps. The Phillipses are co-presidents of the local historical society, and their expertise in period restoration is evident in each of the inn's rooms.

The dining rooms all have working fireplaces and are papered with Victorian prints. The round or square turn-of-the-century oak tables have matching oak chairs. The inn's collection of Victorian hand-embroidered linens is used daily, and there are plants around all of the dining rooms. Service here is formal, in the Victorian tradition, with waiters dressed in ruffled shirts, vests, bow ties, and black trousers, while waitresses wear long Victorian-style dresses with ruffles and long sleeves.

Meals are prepared by Mary Phillips and her staff. The menu, changed weekly, features a choice of six entrées daily with beef, fish or seafood, poultry, lamb, pork, and a crepe offering available each night. On Sunday a four-course brunch is served. A typical dinner might begin with a choice of smoked Lake Superior whitefish or stuffed mushrooms followed by the entrée, which, if a fish dinner were the choice, might be stuffed Lake Superior trout with the vegetables of the day. Accompanying the entrée would be the daily breads such as onion dill or orange walnut. Salad might be wild blackberries and blueberries, strawberries, and bananas in a French cream dressing. The dessert to accompany this meal might be a pot de crème. The meals are both Continental and regional in style, and Mary relies heavily on local produce and the fresh local fish when either is available.

The Phillipses have restored five guest rooms on the second floor, the only ones now available for overnight guests. Three rooms have working fireplaces. The inn has one person that devotes full time to keeping the fires tended in the public and guest rooms. Each room has a turn-of-the-century four-poster bed with a matching dresser. On the bed are hand-crocheted bedspreads and quilts. Each room has a generous supply of books, one or two rockers, and a view of Lake Superior, which is just two blocks away. As on the first floor, the Phillips collection of Victorian lamps is amply represented. A table is often set in each room, so guests who wish to enjoy a romantic candle-lit dinner before their own fireplace may do so. A complimentary bottle of wine and a pair of wine glasses await the arriving guests.

Accommodations: 5 rooms, 2 with private bath. *Pets and children:* Pets are not permitted and children are not encouraged. *Driving Instructions:* Bayfield is on Route 13, 70 miles east of Duluth.

THE GRIFFIN INN

Ellison Bay, WI 54201. 414-854-4306. *Innkeepers:* Paul and Joyce Crittenden. Open all year except April and November.

The Griffin Inn, a gambrel-roofed, shuttered white building, was constructed in 1921. When its current owners bought the place they set out to create a New England–style inn in Wisconsin's Door County. The downstairs lounge has a stone fireplace faced by upholstered furniture including a number of Queene Anne–style pieces. The spacious dining room has a potbellied stove, English buffet, pump organ, and washstand among its many antique pieces. Here hearty country breakfasts are served, and lunch and New England–style five-course dinners are served during the winter months, when the inn is particularly popular with cross-country skiiers. Guests can come in from a day on the cross-country trails or from skating on the lake to warm themselves before the wood-burning stove in the Ski Haus on the property.

The entire inn is filled with handmade things including crewelwork, embroidery, paper quilling, oil paintings, and Oriental rugs. All the guest rooms upstairs are quaintly decorated, many with handmade quilts on antique beds. In addition to the rooms in the inn, there are four cottage units.

The inn has its own apple orchard, which is the source of an abundance of homemade apple sauce, cider, and home-baked apple pies. Fishing, boating, and sandy-beach swimming are within walking distance, and the many other attractions of Wisconsin's Door County are within a short drive. Door County has more miles of shoreline than any other in the nation, as well as the largest inland shipbuilding port. In many ways the county combines the best of New England and the fjord country of Norway.

Accommodations: 10 rooms with shared bath and 4 cottages with private bath. *Pets:* Permitted in cottages only. *Driving Instructions:* From Milwaukee, take I-43 north to Manitowoc and Route 42 to Ellison Bay. In the village, turn right on Mink River Road and drive 2 blocks to the inn.

WHITE GULL INN

Box 175, Fish Creek, WI 54212. 414-868-3517. *Innkeepers:* Andy and Jan Coulson. Open mid-May through late October.

The White Gull Inn, a white clapboard house, looks as if it came off a Vermont mountain and ended up on the shore of Green Bay. According to local historians, the White Gull Inn was brought in one piece to Fish Creek from Marinette, Wisconsin, 18 miles across the bay. This feat was accomplished in the dead of winter with the help of a team of sturdy horses, some huge logs, and a very determined new owner, Dr. Weckler.

White Gull is one of the last historic old Door County inns still in existence. The main section was built in 1896; the dining room and kitchen were added in the 1940s and expanded in 1978. The inn has wide second-floor verandas and a ground-floor porch with old deacon's benches, a cider press, and a bulletin-board of community events and sales. The inn has four small, old-fashioned cottages for families, one with housekeeping facilities. The furnishings at White Gull are what one would expect to find at an old turn-of-the-century country inn; many original pieces are still in residence, along with informal Victorian antiques of the period. The rooms have high ceilings, bare wood floors with scatter rugs, and period print wallpapers. The large lobby has a huge fireplace, the focal point of the room.

The bedrooms are furnished and decorated with country antiques, including old oak and walnut bureaus and old iron bedsteads painted white. The beds all have new mattresses and box springs. Rooms have a restful absence of television, phones, and air conditioning.

White Gull Inn is famous for its Door County Fish Boil, which features fresh lake fish, boiled potatoes, homemade coleslaw, hot breads, and mugs of local or imported beers, topped off with a wedge of home-baked cherry pie. Guests sit on the terrace while the Master Boiler, Russ Ostrand, prepares the dinner over a roaring fire and entertains with his accordion at the same time. The dinner, a Midwest version of the New England clambake, is served rain or shine on Wednesday, Friday, Saturday, and Sunday evenings. Reservations must be made well in advance—this is a very popular attraction. The

inn also has on Monday and Thursday nights an Early American Buffet that rivals the fish boil in popularity. It offers a selection of old-fashioned dishes and fresh baked goods. A typical buffet consists of turkey dumpling soup, corn and clam pie (an old Indian dish), glazed baked ham, maple baked carrots, Boston baked beans, scalloped potatoes, homemade breads, and an assortment of salads and desserts including the favorite, Indian pudding. Again, reservations are a must.

Accommodations: 9 rooms, 5 with private bath. *Pets:* Permitted only in the four cottages. *Driving Instructions:* Take Route 42 from either Manitowoc or Sturgeon Bay to Fish Creek (an unincorporated village). In Fish Creek, turn left at the stop sign at the bottom of the hill and go three blocks.

Green Lake, Wisconsin

THE HEIDEL HOUSE RESORT
AND CONFERENCE CENTER

Illinois Avenue, Green Lake, WI 54941. 414-294-3344. *Innkeepers:* Brent and Brian Heidel. Open all year.

Arriving at Heidel House is a little like arriving at a country village. As in most villages, the buildings represent a variety of architectural styles, ranging in this case from contemporary motel units to mid-nineteenth-century restored and converted houses. The focus of the resort and the building the most like a country inn is Heidel House itself. Here, in 1945, Herb and Lucille Heidel first opened their restaurant on what had been the Kelly estate on the north shore of Green Lake. Respectively a former newspaper publisher and schoolteacher, Herb and Lucille invited guests to stay in four bedrooms on the second floor of the building and enjoy simple, home-cooked meals. Today, the resort comprises 20 acres and more than eight buildings and is managed by the Heidel's twin sons, Brent and Brian.

More than half of the resort's guest rooms are located in the Mariner Lodge, a two-story motel unit with appropriate furnishings that also contains the indoor swimming pool and saunas. Those preferring more traditional accommodations may choose from a variety of remodeled buildings. Grey Rock Mansion, for example, has seven bedrooms, five baths, a winding staircase, and a large living room with two fireplaces. The exterior of the Carriage House—where the estate's horses and carriages were kept—was untouched during renovation that created seven bedrooms and a meeting room. The Guest House has now been converted into a small hotel with eleven guest rooms and two fireplaces. The Pump House that once supplied water to the estate retains its name but is now a luxurious honeymoon suite with bedroom, living room, kitchen, and its own fireplace. Guests making reservations should specify the kind of accommodation they wish. The use of the resort by conference groups sometimes limits the number of rooms available in the traditional buildings.

Dining facilities at Heidel House have expanded greatly over the years. The formal main dining room with its linen service and Continental cuisine offers veal Oscar, chateaubriand, roast duckling Grand Marnier, lobster Thermidor, beef bourguignonne, tournedos en brochette, and seafood and steak entrées, as well as several moderately-priced poultry and chop items. On the floor below is the Rathskeller, and over the inn's circular drive is the Fondue Chalet, which serves exclusively fondue dinners amid Swiss décor.

Resort activities at Heidel House include sauna, whirlpool, an indoor swimming pool, and boating, fishing, riding, tennis, and nearby golf at three eighteen-hole courses. Excursions are offered on spring-fed Green Lake aboard the inn's yacht. Guests may also register for charter-fishing boats. In winter the inn is a cross-country skiing center with trails through the surrounding 1,100 acres. The snow season is also popular for ice fishing and snowmobiling nearby.

Accommodations: 93 rooms, 86 with private bath. *Pets:* Not permitted. *Driving Instructions:* The resort is 28 miles west of Fond du Lac on Route 23 in Green Lake.

Lewis, Wisconsin

SEVEN PINES LODGE AND TROUT PRESERVE

P.O. Box 104, Route 35, Lewis, WI 54851. 715-653-2323. *Innkeepers:* Joan and David Simpson. Open all year.

Seven Pines Lodge, a national historic site, is an idyllic country retreat. It was built in 1903 as a private estate by Charles Lewis, a prominent financier. The hand-hewn-log buildings are surrounded by acres of virgin white pine. The parklike grounds immediately around the lodge are reminiscent of a German forest: manicured and tidy with lawns sweeping down to a trout stream. The lodge, constructed by Norwegian craftsmen imported by Mr. Lewis, has exterior walls of logs; but this is no ordinary log cabin. It is the luxuriously appointed, year-round estate of a wealthy man who wanted a secluded haven for his family and friends. Mr. Lewis's guests were famous and powerful people, including presidents and foreign diplomats. The lodge was sold as a private club, and the Simpsons still run it that way. Guests have the option of becoming members, entitling them and their friends to unlimited use of lodge facilities.

Calvin Coolidge enjoyed staying at the lodge. His presidential suite is Seven Pines's most impressive bedroom, with original décor and French doors opening to the sounds of the whispering pines and the nearby stream. The lodge itself retains all the elegantly rustic furnishings of Mr. Lewis's time. The east porch, overlooking the stream and lawns, still is decked out with Victorian-looking ferns and antique wicker with old-fashioned floral cushions. Time appears to have stopped in the early 1900s. The living room and dining room appear to be untouched. Teddy Roosevelt would feel right at home. There are comfortable-looking upholstered chairs and couches, mission furniture, and other oak pieces. A moosehead surveys the room from the wall above the wide brick fireplace, where fires are always burning when it's chilly. The many mementoes, Oriental rugs, and fringed lampshades harken back to a more easygoing life-style.

Guests have the choice of lodgings in one of three log structures on the grounds. The lodge has five rooms, including the presidential suite, several twin-bedded rooms sharing a large common bath, and a loft with four single beds. The Gate House, once Mr. Lewis's private office, is now a guesthouse surrounded by 100-foot-high pines. It has a working fireplace and four beds and a bath. All rooms are decorated with Mr. Lewis's mementoes. The Stream House is quite an experience. It is across a footbridge and looks for all the world like a log mushroom.

Seven Pines offers recreational activities all year. There are 1,000 acres for secluded hikes and cross-country skiing. The stream is stocked with rainbow and brook trout from the breeding pond, and the surrounding area has hundreds of lakes for boating and fishing.

The lodge's dining room is open to guests for all meals and to the public for lunch and dinner by reservation only. The house specialty is the freshly caught trout. Guests wishing to enjoy their own day's catch can do so in style. The kitchen will prepare it any way one wishes.

Accommodations: 7 rooms, 3 with private bath. *Driving Instructions:* The lodge is 1 mile east of Lewis, which is equidistant from Siren and Frederic on Route 35.

CHATEAU MADELEINE

P.O. Box 27, La Pointe (Madeline Island), WI 54850. *Off-season:* 4209 Country Club Road, Minneapolis, MN 55424. 715-747-2463. *Innkeeper:* Margaret N. Vennum. Open June through mid-October.

Château Madeleine, a romantic island estate, was built in the early 1900s as the summer home of Cora Abernathy Hull of Kansas City. It was called Coolepark Manor. Some thirty years ago the home, grounds, and adjacent cottages were purchased by Margaret Vennum; she has operated it ever since as the island's only inn. It is encompassed by pines and northern birch on a hillside overlooking Lake Superior and the distant Wisconsin mainland. The peaceful estate occupies 15 woodland acres.

The Château's bright rooms are furnished with period antiques that reflect the charm of Cora Hull's time. The rooms' polished hardwood floors and unpainted wainscoting create a summery atmosphere, further enhanced by the lake vistas from the large picture windows. The dining room looks out over the lake to the mainland hills. It is furnished with clear primary colors—bright blue wooden chairs, yellow placemats, and fresh bouquets of flowers on the tables. Just off this room is the second-floor sun deck with its colorful umbrella tables and canvas director's chairs.

Meals offered here have been acclaimed by many local and national publications. The Château operates solely on full American Plan, serving breakfast, lunch, and dinner to its guests; a picnic lunch will be packed at guests' request. Meals are also served to the public with advance reservations. A single entrée is offered each meal, and no menu is printed up. Specialties include roast Cornish game hens on saffron rice, leg of lamb with sour cream gravy, fresh broiled lake trout, and whitefish deep-fried in beer batter. The fresh fish are featured in the popular Monday fish fry held around a campfire on the inn's private sandy beach. Other treats at mealtime are the caramel rolls.

The living room and breakfast room both have attractive tiled fireplaces. Most of the public rooms and two of the guest rooms in the lodge look out over the lake. The rest have views of the forests. On the

sandy beach below the main house is Sea Cottage. Its three guest rooms are pine-paneled with views of Chequamegon Bay. Two other cottages accommodate families and their friends; one has its own private beach. One family-style cottage has a daybed in the living room and a large screened porch with old-fashioned porch swing. The other offers a main section and two wings that may be rented as a unit or separately. There are private decks and a living room with a large working fireplace.

The Château and the beauty of the island offer a special appeal to guests craving solitude and unspoiled natural surroundings. At this unusual spot all of the Apostle Islands and their national lake shore beckon.

Accommodations: 7 rooms in the lodge; 3 cottages with 3 bedrooms each; most with private bath, except the suites. *Pets:* Not permitted. *Children:* Reduced family rate for children under twelve. *Driving Instructions:* The Château can be reached by the fifteen-minute car ferry from Bayfield, Wisconsin, to the town of La Pointe on Madeline Island. The Château is 1½ miles to the right of the town dock. An airstrip on the island is used for flight service from Saint Paul's airport.

JAMIESON HOUSE

407 North Franklin Avenue, Poynette, WI 53955. 608-635-4100.
Innkeeper: Jeff Smith. Open all year. Open for dining Wednesday
through Sunday.

June and Jeff Smith have achieved what most people would consider
the impossible. They have taken over two fine Victorian houses and
created a country inn and gourmet restaurant miles away from the
beaten track. The Smiths purchased the 1878 brick home of Hugh
Jamieson and the 1883 brick home of his son, Hugh Pierce Jamieson,
across the street. The father's house was carefully restored to its
Victorian splendor, employing only true restoration techniques—such
as plastering where others might let sheet rock suffice—and repairing
the ornamental plaster mouldings. The result is a house with three intimate dining rooms on the first floor and the residence for the innkeepers and family on the second.

Diners enter the Jamieson House through a reception room that
once served as Hugh Jamieson's private office. Coats are hung in the
former vault room just off the old office. The room harks to an earlier
day when there were no banks in Poynette. The Gold Dining Room,
the largest of the three, has an unusual Chickering Square grand
piano. This is but one of many musical instruments in Jeff Smith's
collection, reflecting the interest in music that inspired him to obtain a
master's degree in pipe organs. The room, named for its gold wallpapers, has four tables surrounded by Hitchcock chairs. The Cranberry Room, adjacent, has an extensive collection of early Cranberry
glass, displayed in a corner cupboard, and two polished walnut tables.
The third dining room, the Green room, originally the parlor, has
three dining tables.

The guest house across the street contains two-room suites and
double rooms. Each is provided with carefully selected Victorian
antiques in elegant settings. Perhaps the most lavish is the Master
Suite, which has reproduction Victorian blue and green wall cover-
ings, a high-backed rare walnut bed, a marble-top dresser, and, in the
full bathroom, a six-foot sunken tub surrounded by mirrors. The
adjacent sitting room has a velvet antique chaise. Parlour Suite is
done in greens and whites and is noted for its east-facing bay window

Jamieson House

and a bath surrounded by Spanish tiles. In all, the rooms are a perfect complement to the setting at the restaurant. They have no television and no telephone, but all are fully carpeted except the somewhat less formal Sun Room Suite, the only one of the five where smoking is permitted. Included in the room rate is a complete breakfast of any choice from the menu at Sophy's Bib and Tucker Restaurant in the center of Poynette. Sophy's is another project that the Smiths have undertaken with their usual skill and enthusiasm. Many guests like to vary their dining while at Jamieson House by eating some of their meals at this interesting restaurant in the former Jamieson Bank Building.

Accommodations: 4 rooms with private bath. *Driving Instructions:* Poynette is about 25 miles north of Madison. Take I-90 and 94 north to Route 60 east to Route 51 north. Route 51 leads to the outskirts of Poynette. Take the third left onto Hudson Street, which runs past Jamieson House.

Sister Bay, Wisconsin

HOTEL DU NORD

11000 Bay Shore Drive, Sister Bay, Wisconsin. Mailing address: P.O. Box 68, Sister Bay, WI 54234. 414-854-4221. *Innkeepers:* Keyes and Ardis Fletcher. Open mid-May to early November plus Christmas, Thanksgiving and weekends in January and February. Hotel du Nord is a fine old country hotel overlooking a bay. The buildings are French Canadian architecture surrounded by woods, lawns, and water. The original building was commissioned in 1916 by Josephine Anderson, who thought Door County would make an ideal vacation spot and turned out to be 100 percent correct. In those good old days, Miss Anderson's rate schedule was $2.50 per person for a room and three hearty meals. The hotel was enlarged in 1920 and extensively remodeled in 1954 and 1971, when the main house and dining room were winterized. In 1978 a lodge was added, bringing the number of guest rooms up to thirty-one, each with a modern bath. The hotel is on 5 acres of woodsy property with open waterfront visible from the lawns, some of the guest rooms, and the dining room. The waterfront area offers a pier, a private sandy beach, and a sun deck for guests.

Some of the guest rooms open onto the balcony overlooking the lobby. These and other guests' quarters in the lodge are furnished traditionally but manage to keep up the general flavor. Various antiques belonging to the Fletchers and some that have been here since Miss Anderson's days are blended into the décor of the rooms. Downstairs, guests relax and visit or read in front of the fire or join a card game in progress at one of the tables set up around the room. The cocktail lounge, highlighted by antique stained-glass windows, is informal.

The dining room, called the Back Room, serves traditional American hotel fare with a salad buffet, grilled steaks, and seafoods. The specialties are Shrimp du Nord, skewered bacon-wrapped shrimp served on wild rice pilaf; broiled whitefish fresh from the nearby waters; and roast boneless Wisconsin duckling on a bed of wild rice with natural gravy. On Sunday a buffet brunch from 9 A.M. to 1 P.M. is open to the public, as are all meals here.

Accommodations: 31 rooms with private bath. *Pets:* Not permitted. *Driving Instructions:* The hotel is a mile north of Sister Bay on Bay Shore Drive (Route 42).

Sturgeon Bay, Wisconsin

BAY SHORE INN

Bay Shore Drive, Sturgeon Bay, WI 54235. 414-743-4551. *Innkeepers:* The Hansons and the Mathiases. Open May through October.

The Bay Shore Inn is a resort on the bay in scenic Door County, Wisconsin. It contains just about every conceivable type of accommodation, but the emphasis is on more contemporary lodging in A-frame or beachfront cottages of recent vintage. The inn has grown up out of an old orchard farm. In 1922 the barn that served the apple industry on the farm was converted into what is now the main lodge. The dining room there still retains the original hardwood floor from its apple storage days. The lodge has an early American atmosphere, with a fireplace in the lobby, couches, rockers, and books scattered about in a homey fashion. Upstairs in the lodge seven old-fashioned guest rooms, with sinks but sharing a hall bath, appeal to those who seek a family-oriented, innlike atmosphere.

Also appealing for their historic atmosphere are the Farmhouse rooms. The Farmhouse, built in 1880, is a small and cheerful one-and-a-half-story cottage with a recently added kitchen wing. Much of the original furniture from the last century remains in the three guest rooms (two are suites) available here. The remaining lodgings are offered in the screened-porched Beach Terrace cabins, the Ranch Terraces that face the orchard, six A-frame Chalet cottages, and a two-bedroom cottage called Woodside. All the cabins have contemporary furnishings; most have views of the bay.

The Bayshore was originally developed by John and Matilda Hanson, immigrants from Sweden. The inn's early fame came from the Swedish recipes used by Matilda in her kitchen, many of which are still used by the Hanson children, who currently run the inn. The inn maintains its own garden, which supplies many of its vegetables during the summer season. Breakfasts at the Bayshore offer not only the expected cereals and eggs but special Swedish pancakes served with a dish of lingonberries. The breads served at breakfast and throughout the day are all homemade, as are the jellies and jams. At dinner the inn offers four regular items, including steak, ground sirloin, broiled fillet of Lake Michigan whitefish, and a chef's salad. Each day there is a daily special, which may be prime ribs, pork chops, roast chicken or lamb, steak kabobs, or barbecued ribs. Soup is served daily, and a particular house specialty is the cheese soup. On Friday evenings the inn offers a traditional Door County fish boil, consisting of boiled fish and potatoes, salad, relish tray, breads, and donuts. The fish boil is served in the early evening on the beach.

Recreational facilities at the Bayshore include a game room in the lodge and a larger separate recreation hall by the beach that offers table tennis, pool, fooz ball, pinball, card tables, and a jukebox. The main focus of attention is on the bay, with swimming, sailing, water skiing, and fishing available at the beachfront. There is a screened outdoor tennis court for guests.

Accommodations: 30 rooms, 23 with private bath. *Pets:* Not permitted. *Driving Instructions:* Enter Sturgeon Bay on Business Route 42-57 and cross the bridge. Immediately turn left onto First Avenue. Follow First past the shipyards to the intersection of Iowa and Third Avenue. Turn left on Third (also called Bay Shore Drive and County Road B). The inn is 3 miles from the city at 4205 Bay Shore Drive.

Iowa

Keosauqua, Iowa

MANNING HOTEL

Keosauqua, IA 52565. 319-293-3232. *Innkeepers:* Dick, Mary, Mike, and Sally Mairet. Open all year.

Lovers of old country inns all have their own special place hidden somewhere off the beaten track. The Manning Hotel is Iowa's special place. It is a restored old riverboat hotel on the banks of the Des Moines River. The long second-floor veranda still looks out on the horseshoe bend in the river as if waiting for the steamboats *Clara Dine* and *Charley Rogers* to come chugging up to the dock to discharge their passengers. The historic hotel, now in the National Registry of Historic Places, was built in several stages. The first floor was constructed as a general store and bank in 1854 on the spot where Edwin Manning's log cabin trading post had burned in the early 1850s. Manning arrived here in 1837 and, three years later, built the first brick courthouse west of the Mississippi on a hill above his store. The second and third stories were added by Manning in the late 1890s, when he transformed the building into a hotel and restaurant serving the riverboat trade. The hotel has been in operation ever since.

In 1961 six rooms were added in a motel unit next to the hotel, and in 1977 the Mairet family began the complete restoration of the inn to its original state. The furnishings selected by Manning are still in residence here, looking a bit brighter since their refinishing and fresh coats of paint. The entire hotel appears to be just as Manning left it.

There are print wallpapers, the woodwork in the rooms and halls has been stripped and cleaned, and many of the windows have the original interior shutters on them. The polished wood floors are covered with brightly colored braided scatter rugs. The lobby has the original lighting fixtures, display cases, heavy oak furniture, and a staircase leading up to the guest rooms.

The guest rooms are slowly being restored. Eight, including two popular honeymoon suites, have already been completely redone: Besides the wood's being stripped and cleaned, the old wicker has been given a fresh coat of paint and the ornately carved Victorian beds, dressers, chairs, and tables have been refinished and waxed. All the beds are covered with antique quilts. One room has twin double beds of scrolled white iron and brass with cushioned white wicker chairs, a wicker table, and potted plants in front of a bank of tall windows opening onto the veranda. Another room has two Jenny Lind spool beds, both doubles, old Victorian rockers, and a desk overlooking the river through the veranda's white pillars. About twelve other comfortable rooms are rented for less because they have not yet been restored.

In the hotel's dining room there are plants everywhere, and the white-clothed tables have groupings of antique bentwood chairs around them. The door has a brightly colored stained-glass transom, and the each window is topped with stained-glass panels. Old photos and prints decorate the wallpapered walls, and the old lighting fixtures still light the room in the evenings. The breakfasts and lunches are hearty Iowa meals cooked with fresh local ingredients in season. Dinners begin with hot homemade soups such as the special cheese soup, or minestrone, a potato soup, a vegetable soup, or whatever strikes the chef's fancy. Traditional American home-style cooking is a favorite with local Iowans and visitors from all over. The Manning serves roast beef with gravy, mashed potatoes, and green beans or peas; a scalloped seafood casserole; or a big portion of roast chicken or Iowa pork with all the fixings. The special is steak Diane smothered with mushrooms in wine sauce. Home-baked breads and a salad bar accompany all meals. The desserts are fresh-baked pies and ice cream.

Accommodations: 22 rooms, 14 with private bath. *Driving Instructions:* Keosauqua is on Route 1 in the southeast corner of Iowa, quite near the borders of Missouri and Illinois.

Amana Colonies—Homestead, Iowa

Early in the eighteenth century a group of inspirationists (German Lutheran separatists) immigrated to this country and eventually settled on thousands of acres of Iowa farmland. They founded seven communal villages known as the Amana Colonies, which are going strong today, although most of the community property has been redistributed as stock and the villagers own their own homes. Farming is still the main industry, but Amana is famous nationwide for a number of products, primarily Amana refrigerators and ranges. Quality of workmanship has made Amana baked goods, hand-crafted furniture, and clocks much sought after. Most of their bakeries, wineries, clock and furniture factories, craft shops, and more are open for public tours.

DIE HEIMAT MOTOR HOTEL

Amana Colonies, Homestead, IA 52236. 319-622-3937. *Innkeepers:* Jim and Barbara Lloyd. Open all year except three weeks in January.

Die Heimat, a restored building that has been caring for travelers since 1854, is in Homestead, one of the seven villages that make up the historic Amana Colonies of Iowa. Each village had a communal kitchen providing meals for the villagers, but in 1932 the colonies gave up their communal way of life during the Great Change, and the kitchens were closed. Die Heimat was the kitchen house of Homestead; when that operation closed it became a private home that sometimes provided lodging for overnight guests and boarders. In the 1960s it was bought by two enterprising Amana men who gutted the old building and redesigned the interior to include a lounge and guest rooms with private baths. The exterior was given a face-lift but remains relatively unchanged from its clean Amana architectural lines. Each room has its own personality and décor, with carpets and double beds. The rooms' beds, chairs, sofas, and accessory furniture are manufactured in the colonies at the Amana Furniture Shops. In 1975 the present innkeepers, Jim and Barbara Loyd, bought the inn and added three larger guest rooms that feature air conditioning, wet bar, and (what else?) an Amana refrigerator. The lobby and guest rooms are decorated with art by local Amana people, some family

heirlooms, and German "house blessings" reflecting the religious nature of the colonies. Some of the old proverbs were brought from Germany well over a hundred years ago. The inviting lounge, completely furnished with such attractive Amana pieces as upholstered rockers and love seats, has an Amana grandfather clock as its focal point. Guests enjoy gathering here for friendly conversation in the evening. Another social time is at the breakfast table over hot coffee and rolls, toast, and juice. This complimentary breakfast is the only meal offered at Die Heimat, but Jim and Barbara will gladly steer hungry guests to the nearby restaurants featuring Amana's famous German dishes.

Jim Loyd's voice is familiar to many Iowans who remember him from his days on Cedar Rapids radio. Now Jim and Barbara devote themselves to their guests and the inn. This attention certainly shows; Die Heimat is neat as a pin inside and out. The name "Die Heimat" translates from German loosely into "The Home Place" but more clearly conveys "You are home."

Accommodations: 18 rooms with private bath. *Pets:* Not permitted. *Driving Instructions:* Take either Route 149 south from Cedar Rapids or Route 6 west of Iowa City to Homestead.

Mount Pleasant, Iowa

HARLAN HOUSE

122 North Jefferson Street, Mount Pleasant, IA 52641. 319-385-3126. *Innkeeper:* J.W. McMillan. Open all year.

The 1857 portion of Harlan House is sandwiched between two sections that were added at the turn of the century when the original residence was converted to a hotel. The hotel is an ivy-covered brick building with white wood trim and a pillared entrance. The ivy almost completely hides the brick and even reaches over some of the windows. This is an old-fashioned Midwestern small-town establishment in the best tradition. The middle section of the hotel was once the home of Senator John Harlan, a close friend of Lincoln's and father-in-law to Lincoln's eldest son. The young Lincolns inherited the house and later sold it to be a hotel. The original part of the house contains a dining room used for private parties. This Lincoln-Harlan Room has been restored and contains a working fireplace, period furnishings, and many interesting mementos of the hotel's early days.

The large lobby contains desks, lounging chairs, and television set for guests, and a big fireplace where fires are lit on chilly days and nights. The centerpiece of the room is an old Regulator grandfather's clock. The lobby also has a bus depot, a travel agency, and a gift shop. Off the lobby are the only ground-floor guest quarters, a spacious suite of rooms with a private bath. The second and third floors contain the rest of the guest rooms, most using old-fashioned hall bathrooms. The hotel's décor changed only gradually with the times until the late 1940s. Here it remains; the comfortable, high-ceilinged, papered rooms are redolent of an earlier time.

The dining room downstairs offers Iowa dishes to travelers, guests, and townspeople every day but Sunday. The menu changes daily and features a wide variety of "down home" cooking with platters of roast beef, pork, beef stews, beef and noodle casseroles, meatloaf, hamloaf, pork chops, and—every Friday—fish. The house favorite is the big bowl of home-made soup; one kind invariably comes with each day of the week; Mondays it is vegetable; Tuesdays, cream of potato, and so on. The other "constant" is lemon pie every Saturday; for more than thirty years people have flocked here on Saturdays to have a slice or two or three of the Harlan House lemon pie.

Accommodations: 40 rooms, 14 with private bath, and a suite.
Driving Instructions: The hotel is 27 miles west of Burlington (on the Mississippi River) on Route 34 in the heart of Mount Pleasant.

Kansas

Ashland, Kansas

HARDESTY HOUSE

712 Main Street, Ashland, KS 67831. 316-635-2911. *Innkeepers:* Betty, Edith, and Jack Hardesty. Open all year.

Hardesty House is a two-story brick, tile, and concrete hotel dating back to the early 1900s. The hotel, which has been maintained by two generations of the Hardesty family, welcomes guests today with room after room of turn-of-the-century furnishings. When you enter the lobby, you see a wide stairway to the second floor. A cashier's cage from an early bank, old rockers, benches, and a hat tree establish the period flavor. Hanging from the lobby walls are pictures of people and events from the Ashland area's past, as well as kerosene lamps with metal reflectors. There is an ornate old heating stove that still functions, although it has been converted to gas for convenience. The old-fashioned wallpaper and the pressed-tin ceilings, complete with metal faces in the corners, reinforce the feeling of yesteryear.

There are two dining rooms at Hardesty House. The only meal served to the public is the Sunday buffet, but the rooms are also used for special luncheons, meetings of the Kiwanis Club, wedding receptions, and parties. The larger of two dining rooms features wainscoting of old barn siding (originally painted red and now weathered). More pictures grace these walls, and the ceilings are once again of pressed tin. Above the wainscoting is Victorian-style wallpaper, and several old farm implements are on display in the room. A bearskin rug hangs on one wall, a trophy of an early-day banker. In one corner is an old piano with old-fashioned dolls and kerosene lamps on its top. A cupboard built into the chimney holds the sheet music for the piano. The room has several large ceiling fans that contribute to its ambience and comfort. The tables in this room are covered with red-

checkered cloths. The smaller dining room features old-fashioned wallpaper, perhaps a little fancier in design, and the round oak tables have white linen cloths and are surrounded by antique chairs.

Edith Hardesty, Jack's mother, prepares the food for the Sunday buffet, with the help of a capable staff. The buffet dinner includes such items as skillet-fried chicken, chicken casseroles, sausages and rice, fresh vegetables such as zucchini or cauliflower, and several salads. Prune whip is a frequent dessert, although Christmas buffets often include cranberry fluff instead. Reservations are almost a must.

Off the lobby is a sitting room that features a hanging stained-glass lamp, a Victorian velvet love seat, several rockers, an oak bookcase-and-desk combination, a small "oak heater," a bentwood easel, a magazine rack, more old pictures, and a marble-top occasional table.

Several guest rooms are furnished with brass beds, and one has an early walnut-backed bed. Each has chairs, rockers, and dressers, some marble-topped. The walls are covered with reproduction early American papers, and the baths have either old wooden or other antique mirrors and light fixtures. In addition to regular rooms, there are two apartments. One is a studio room with some antique furnishings; the other has one bedroom, a living room, a kitchen, and a bathroom. Both have air conditioning.

Accommodations: 12 rooms, 8 with private bath. *Pets:* Not permitted. *Driving Instructions:* The hotel is in Ashland on U.S. 160, approximately 50 miles southeast of Dodge City, Kansas.

BEAUMONT HOTEL

Route K-96, Beaumont, Kansas. Mailing Address: P.O. Box 20, Beaumont, KN 67012. 316-843-2242. *Innkeepers:* John, Tom, and Pete Savute. Open all year except Christmas.

The Beaumont Hotel was established in 1879 by the Saint Louis and San Francisco Railroad, which was then under construction. In the 1880s close to one hundred railroad employees stayed at the hotel while they maintained the roundhouse and the freight and ticket offices at the Beaumont station. Across from the Beaumont in those days were holding pens for 9,000 cattle, shipped to the area to fatten on Kansas bluestem grass, one of the richest cattle grasses in the country. Four eastbound and four westbound trains each day brought cattle and cattlemen from Oklahoma, Texas, and New Mexico to the town, then took them out to the markets with their fattened livestock. In those days, Beaumont was a ripsnorting wild West town that boasted three barber shops (including one in the hotel), a doctor's office, a blacksmith shop, a bank, and a post office. The potboiling steam-powered trains would chug into town breathing sparks and slow to a halt at the wooden water tower to refill their water tanks. (At that time, steam trains required refills from such towers every 50 miles or so.) The original Beaumont tower, one of the few to survive the demise of the steam trains, still stands not far from the hotel.

In the 1940s a rancher from New Mexico asked if he could land his plane in town and was told that a suitable field lay to the east of the hotel. This marked the beginning of a tradition of welcoming small planes at the landing strip adjacent to the building. Each year hundreds of planes fly in to practice turf landings and enjoy the hotel's fine Kansas cooking. The à la carte menu offers catfish, ham, turkey, baked steak, several grilled steaks, a choice of three Italian dishes, and several sandwiches.

Over the years the hotel has been expanded and modernized, but many old-fashioned touches remain. During one renovation in the 1950s the hotel barbershop was removed, but the original mirrored back wall still exists in what is now a private dining room. The upstairs bedrooms were remodeled and several baths were added (the town had no running water in the nineteenth century), as was a central heating system. Some guest rooms now have brass beds, others have modern furniture, and all have air conditioning. The hotel's Western décor includes airplane photos, knotty-pine paneling, wide-board plank floors, and pictures of Beaumont as it was during the cattle days.

Accommodations: 12 rooms, 6 with private bath. *Pets:* Not permitted. *Driving Instructions:* Beaumont is 40 miles due east of Wichita on Route K-96.

Harper, Kansas

ROSALEA'S HOTEL
121 West Main Street, Harper, KS 67058. No telephone; write for reservations. *Innkeeper:* Rosalea. Open May 1 through Labor Day.

If you are the sort of reader who hastily skims through a description, you might take time to read through the following from beginning to end before racing off to Harper to book a room at Rosalea's unusual enterprise. Rosalea's defies easy description. It is literally a hotel in a small Kansas town. Built in 1883 of 26-inch-thick limestome blocks, it survived an awesome tornado in 1893 and became an important staging place for people joining the land rush to Oklahoma three years later. The historical description could continue, but it is Rosalea's that demands attention.

Rosalea bought her hotel, then in sagging condition, in 1968, after she had completed college and spent three years as a professional artist in New York City. At $1,500 it was probably a bargain, although the aches—heartache, backache, soul ache—that followed would be hard to place a dollar value on. Rosalea almost immediately found herself the object of a chilly reception by Harper's citizens. She can produce a file of more than thirty newspaper articles chronicling her struggles with a community that saw her and her guests as a "hippie haven" that had somehow descended on Harper.

Rosalea asserts that a hotel can be a humanizing experience as well as a comfortable place to stay. As she says, "There is never a condemnation of one's sexual preference, beliefs, race, or age. Guests are treated as people, not room numbers.... Rosalea's Hotel is not for

everyone.... In fact you won't be comfortable at Rosalea's Hotel
unless you can cope with walking one block to use a telephone and
remembering to lock the front door (to keep the sightseer out) or
unless you can appreciate the foil-and-magazine-collage décor (there
being no money for the more traditional wallpaper or paint). But the
peaceful, casual comfort of Rosalea's Hotel does appeal to many
people of quality—sensitive intellectuals, eccentrics, writers, musi-
cians, artists, actors, dancers and people who are caught in The
System, but wish they weren't.''

Rosalea's vision has come up against Harper bureaucracy; as a
result, and to maintain an atmosphere hinted at above, she has set up
some rather complex rules about staying at the hotel. To protect
everything, she has no telephone; you must therefore write for a
reservation. But you are not allowed to make a room reservation
unless you are a supporting member of the Hotel. Membership dues
range from $10 to $1,000. The former, the basic household membership, allows you to book a room (for the member and a limited
number of guests) during the membership year. Included with
membership are tidbits of Rosalea memorabilia including the hand-
cut autographed black snowflake for which she has become famous.
Members are also invited to Treat M.E.E.T.s (Members' Exciting
and Eccentric Treats) held throughout the year. Some recent ones
included a caviar and champagne gourmet breakfast in the hayloft of
an old barn, a wine-and-cheese-tasting party on the Salt Plains Flats,
and a midnight watermelon feed in an old cemetery on a night with a
full moon. The $1000 Eternal Life Membership conveys a "blizzard"
of black snowflakes, the privilege of renting the whole hotel on a

space-available basis for eternity, and free lodging for the member's spirit after death. Membership funds are earmarked for special building restoration projects. Past funds produced a new roof and rewiring; still needed are new mattresses, exterior repair, and improved plumbing.

As for the rooms, Rosalea gives you a choice when you make your reservation. The simplest she describes as "standard plain, ugly rooms that have made Rosalea's Hotel notorious since 1968." Several of these have brass or iron beds, and all share public showers. The middle-priced rooms are "refreshing collage-and-foil rooms with old-fashioned tub in private bath," while the most costly are "sparkling two-room suites with eclectic décor." Some have tubs; and others, waterbeds.

If all this madness puts you off, the chances are that you would be uncomfortable at Rosalea's. If it seems like fun, it will be. The country is presently caught up in a nostalgic passion for the 1950s. If we are soon to be swept away by memories of the 1960s, Rosalea's is ready.

Accommodations: 12 rooms, some with private bath. *Driving Instructions:* From Wichita, take Route 2-42 southwest to Suppesville, then continue on Route 2 to Harper.

Harper is a town of about 1,800 about 50 miles southwest of Wichita. *Runnymeade Church* was built in 1889 in an English settlement about 10 miles from Harper. The church was moved four years later to Harper, where it still stands as a monument. It is open daily 1:30 to 4:30 except Sunday by appointment. The *Harper Historical Museum* is open Sunday 1 to 5 and by appointment. There is fishing for bass and catfish in Anthony Lake, 7 miles south of town. Country auctions are held frequently in the summer months, and there are a number of antique shops within a 40-mile radius. The public may use the tennis courts at Harper City Park.

Missouri

YE ENGLISH INN
   Downing Street, Hollister, Missouri. Mailing address: P.O. Box
   506, Hollister, MO 65672. 417-334-4142. *Innkeeper:* Maurice John
   Swanberg. Open April through October.

Ye English Inn is part of an unusual Elizabethan-style town in Missouri's Ozarks. Once a primitive frontier wilderness, the area was opened up with the coming of the St. Louis, Iron Mountain, and Southern Railroad. W. T. Johnson's Timber and Real Estate Company mapped out and began the construction of the English-style village to attract visitors to this scenic area on the Turkey Creek and Lake Taneycomo. Mr. Johnson's dream resulted in a row of Elizabethan structures along what is now called Downing Street. His son, W. W. Johnson, built Ye English Inn in 1909. It was soon the center of this village. There were no usable roads at that time, but special trains brought guests to the remote town. The old railroad station still stands, housing the city offices. The railroad was responsible for promoting the inn and the "English Village of the Ozarks" and sponsored many gala festivities, such as grape carnivals during the harvesting of the grapes from nearby vineyards.

The inn is constructed of native fieldstone with stucco upper stories accented by dark wood studs and crossbeams. The inn's interior walls have the same Elizabethan look, with exposed fieldstone and dark beams. The lobby's large stone fireplace is surrounded by rockers and other comfortable couches and chairs. A stone spiral staircase leads from the lobby the second-floor guest rooms and a private sitting lounge for guests' enjoyment. The rooms throughout the inn have undergone renovation and modernization in recent years. The furnishings are fairly modern, so the décor doesn't really pick up the theme of Elizabethan times, but the basic structure remains intact. There is an ivy-wall courtyard enclosing a swimming pool and spacious patio where guests can swim, sun, and enjoy a poolside snack or drink.

Off the rustic lobby is the combination dining room and pub. Family-style meals are served by the fireside, where fires on the stone hearth lend a warmth to the room. Breakfast, lunch, and dinner are available to guests and public alike. The favorite at dinnertime is the innkeeper's individually cut filets. The menu features steaks and fresh Ozark catfish and mountain trout in season. The Old English Pub is the only room that remains open all year long, serving a selection of beer, ale, and mixed drinks.

Accommodations: 21 rooms with private bath. *Pets:* Very small pets permitted. *Driving Instructions:* From Springfield take Route 65 south to Hollister and then left on Business Route 65 to downtown.

THE INN ST. GEMME BEAUVAIS

78 North Main Street, Sainte Genevieve, Missouri. Mailing address: P.O. Box 231, Sainte Genevieve, MO 63670. 314-883-5744. *Innkeepers:* Mr. and Mrs. Norbert Donze. Open all year.

In the late 1840s, Felix Rozier bought property on North Main Street from the Le Clere family and set about building a home designed to withstand the elements for many centuries. The three-story building is made of solid brick, and even the interior walls are 18 inches thick. An early member of the Le Clere family had married the daughter of one Vital St. Gemme Beauvais, and the association between the owners of the property on which the inn now stands and the St. Gemme Beauvais family gave the current innkeepers their name for the inn.

As you step across the broad veranda, its roof supported by six tall columns, you enter the front hall of the inn and immediately face an open staircase leading to the guest rooms above. Hanging in the hall and setting the antique feeling of this restored early building is a four-armed chandelier bearing amber glass shades. The lighting fixture is one of many treasured local antiques collected by the current owners for installation in their inn. It is dated 1849 and was rescued by a local dealer and sold to them. An oak coat tree stands in the hall, and on the floor is ruby-red-and-gold woollen carpeting, complemented by wallpaper that has almost a matching print. Just off the hall is the office papered with traditional pineapple print denoting hospitality. The registration desk is a rolltop type with an old-fashioned spool cabinet on top and a set of post office boxes rescued from an old country store at its side.

The dining room has white walls, and a white marble mantel frames the working fireplace. In the center of the room is a large antique oval table around which are arranged ladderback chairs. In the morning guests assemble here and are served family-style at this or another table. Each day a full breakfast—included in the price of the room —features a great variety of main dishes, among them filled crepes, herb omelets, French toast, and eggs Benedict. For lunch a single entrée is served each day. Among the regulars are quiche Lorraine, chicken-filled crepes, and chicken à la king. The luncheon includes tossed green salad, vegetable, French bread, and dessert. Several

desserts are made but Mrs. Donze is particularly proud of the sherried peach trifle. No dinner is served at the inn, but local restaurants are handy.

Most of the rooms at the inn are private suites of two rooms each, and most are on the second floor, the exceptions being two suites on the ground level and two large rooms on the third floor. The rooms are all decorated with Victorian furniture. Several have coordinated bedroom sets, such as the elaborate mahogany furniture in one room or the oak and walnut sets in two others. Still other rooms have a mixture of woods, but the selection is almost completely Victorian. Half a block from the inn the family has purchased and restored a home, dating from 1770, that has additional guest rooms on the second floor for use when the main inn is full.

Accommodations: 2 rooms and 6 suites, all with private bath. *Pets:* Not permitted. *Driving Instructions:* From Saint Louis travel south on I-55 to Route 32. Exit east on 32 to Route 61. Take 61 to the Sainte Genevieve exit and into town. The inn is on Main Street.

Nebraska

Belgrade, Nebraska

BEL-HORST INN

P.O. Box 205, Belgrade, NB 68623. 308-357-1094. *Innkeepers:* Warren L. Johnson and Grace Anderson. Open all year.

A visit to the Bel-Horst Inn is like a trip back in time. The hotel was built in 1907 in the traditional brick "in-town" hotel style. The Bel-Horst began as the Andrews Hotel and housed a bank, doctor's office, and hardware store on the ground floor in addition to the prosperous restaurant. When the Depression came along, the hotel closed down. It stayed closed for forty years, with all its furnishings and authentic period décor still intact inside. In the early 1970s two brothers from rural Belgrade, Richard and Donald Horst, bought the old hotel and began a three-year-long complete renovation. Everything had to be painted in the original colors of the period and hung with carefully selected wallpapers reproducing the ambience of the early 1900s. The furnishings needed no more than some refinishing and general sprucing up. If the original Andrews Hotel owner were to walk in today, the only "newfangled" changes he'd find would be the private bathrooms and air-conditioning in the rooms and electricity replacing kerosene in the old hall lanterns and chandeliers.

On the lower floor of the hotel are the lobby, a large dining room, a private dining room, the kitchen, and the guests' lounge. These rooms contain many nostalgic items of the past: an antique lavatory with a fluted pedestal sink, a working old-time popcorn machine, a

player piano, and a Victrola. The floral papered walls of the rooms and hallways are covered with hundreds of photos of early Belgrade residents and street scenes. In the dining room one finds sturdy oak chairs and round pedestal tables, an old hutch filled with china, and brass chandeliers with flowers painted on the glass. In one corner of the room stands an old horseless carriage, and a strange antique doll swings from the painted tin ceiling, welcoming guests into the restaurant. Warren Johnson doubles as the hotel's main chef. Dinners and a Sunday brunch buffet are the only meals srved. The fare runs to steaks, prime ribs, and a variety of seafood, such as rainbow trout and lobster tails. The soups, vegetables, and pies and pastries are made from scratch in the hotel kitchen with its antique stove.

The second floor has individually decorated guest rooms. Old-fashioned lace curtains on the windows, antique Victorian brass and wood bedsteads covered with old patchwork quilts, and floral wallpapers work to create a fine period atmosphere where our grandparents would feel right at home.

Accommodations: 14 rooms with private bath. *Pets:* "Well-behaved" small pets are permitted; be sure to check when making a reservation. *Driving Instructions:* From I-80, exit at the Aurora interchange and go 40 miles north on Route 14 to Route 52 west. Go west 5 miles to Belgrade.

FORT ROBINSON STATE PARK LODGE AND CABINS

P.O. Box 392, Crawford, NB 69339. 308-665-2660. *Innkeeper:* Vince Rotherham. Open Memorial Day through Labor Day and on a limited basis thereafter until mid-November.

On September 5, 1877, a proud Indian chief was being led to imprisonment in a small log cabin at Fort Robinson. Suddenly he struggled free, slashing the hand of one of his captors. In an instant another trooper from the fort thrust forward his bayonet, and it found its mark. Thus died the greatest Oglala Sioux chief of recent history, Chief Crazy Horse. The killing of Crazy Horse was but one in a long string of encounters between the army troops and the local Sioux. For many years Fort Robinson remained an important outpost in the developing Nebraska Territory. After World War II it was abandoned by the army and taken over by the State of Nebraska. Today it serves as the center of a state park that includes not only lodging in the many historic fort buildings but several important museums and historical sites.

Overnight lodging is available in a variety of buildings dating from the late-nineteenth and early-twentieth centuries. The largest facility is the lodge, formerly the enlisted men's barracks, built in 1909. The lodge is a two-and-one-half-story brick building with first- and second-floor verandas running the length of the building and bounded by tall columns. The lodge contains twenty-four guest rooms, and a number of cabins on the grounds may be rented by families or groups. The oldest of these are the Adobe Cabins, which date from 1874 and 1875, and the 1887 Officers Quarters. These are housekeeping cabins with baths, utensils, linens, dishes, and silverware service for six. They range from two-bedroom to four-bedroom units. Several other cabins, with and without housekeeping facilities, are from the 1909 building programs and are constructed of brick. The largest are seven-bedroom units and are frequently rented by large groups. A modern campsite area is also on the grounds.

A popular attraction at the park is the Post Playhouse. The theater group presents a season of repertory that includes melodramas (recently presented were *Time Wounds All Heels* and *Frontier Fury, or Treachery at Fort Robinson*) and comedies. *Trailside Museum*, on

the park grounds, shows the natural history of the area. The Fort
Robinson Museum covers the area's history from prehistoric man
through the Indian wars. Displays include the world's largest army
remount depot, an adjutant's office, a guardhouse, and wheelwright,
blacksmith, and harness repair shops. The museum is open April 1 to
November 15. In addition to these attractions there are trail rides,
jeep rides, several organized tours, stagecoach rides, frequent
cookouts, and weekly rodeos.

The dining room in the main lodge serves three meals daily to
guests and the public. The dinner menu includes trout, roast beef,
several steaks, and a variety of seafood.

Accommodations: 24 lodge rooms with private bath. Many cabins
on the grounds. *Driving Instructions:* Fort Robinson is 3½ miles west
of Crawford on Route 20.

North Dakota

HOTEL POWERS

Broadway at Fourth Avenue, Fargo, North Dakota. *Mailing address:* P.O. Box 1958, Fargo, ND 58102. 701-232-2517. *Innkeeper:* Lawrence Powers.

The Hotel Powers is one of a large number of four-square brick in-town hotels built to accommodate the traveling public near the turn of the century. In the days before family motor travel, the Powers, like its sister hotels throughout the country, drew much of its trade from traveling businessmen, salesmen, and the like. Built in 1919 of concrete, tile, and brick, the four-story Powers was touted at the time as a wholly fireproof hotel—no lumber or other flammable materials had been used in its construction. It was put up by the T. F. Powers Company and is still owned and managed by the Powers family. The building is trimmed with cream terra cotta, which is ornately carved along the roof line. The upper portion of the lobby windows are colored leaded glass. Inside the lobby, the most notable feature is the ornate elevator housing. On one side of the lobby the original grandfather clock still keeps perfect time.

One of the first guests to register at the Powers was James J. Hill,

founder and builder of the Great Northern Railroad. Its successor, the Burlington Northern, is still served by the Amtrak "Empire Builder" run. In 1937 the remodeled coffeeshop became a popular meeting place where one could enjoy a hamburger and a milkshake and listen to the first public performances of singer Peggy Lee. Today's shop offers homemade soups, pan-fried hash browns, popovers, several chicken, steak, chop, and shrimp dishes as well as an assortment of sandwiches and specials of the day.

The hotel rooms are generally furnished with early-American-style furniture. Many of the baths still have the original claw-foot, cast-iron tubs. The most recent remodeling has been the conversion of a block of plain rooms to include modern showers. Air conditioning is available, and each room with bath is equipped with television and radio. Parking is available next to the building.

Accommodations: 94 rooms, 57 with private bath. *Driving Instructions:* The hotel is in downtown Fargo, four blocks from business routes I-94 and I-29 as well as U.S. 52 and 81.

Medora, North Dakota

Medora was founded in 1883 when the Marquis de Mores, a French nobleman, cracked a bottle of champagne over a tent peg and proclaimed that the town would forever bear the name of his daughter Medora. De Mores had come to the area earlier to hunt buffalo and bear, as did a more famous American, Theodore Roosevelt. Camped on the banks of the Little Missouri River, de Mores had envisioned an empire that would make him millions almost overnight. He built a meat-packing plant and started to ship dressed beef to stores he opened in large U.S. cities. (Some have speculated that he planned to use the profits to corrupt the French Army and restore the monarchy with himself as emperor.) His first packing plant was completed in October 1883, but his warehouse butchers began to report back to him that the consumers were complaining about the grass-fed beef. Rumors began to spread that his beef contained poisonous preservatives, and in 1886 he slaughtered his last herd. The winter that followed was one of the most grueling in North Dakota history. Many ranchers, including Roosevelt, were nearly or entirely wiped out. By the 1890s Medora was little more than a ghost town.

Today, Medora has been restored mostly through the the the efforts of one man, Howard Schafer, president of the Gold Seal Wax Company. With headquarters in Bismarck, Schafer had for many years been drawn to the Badlands surrounding Medora. Finally he sought to locate the principal holders of the property in Medora. After an extensive search he located the living heirs to the marquis's property, then residing in Biarritz. The grandson of the marquis was finally persuaded to sell his holdings in Medora to the Gold Seal Company, and restoration work began in earnest. Almost all of the chief attractions in the town are owned and operated by the company.

ROUGH RIDERS HOTEL

Main Street, Medora, North Dakota. Mailing address: P.O. Box 198, Medora, ND 58645. 701-623-4444 or 800-437-2070. *Innkeeper:* John Conway. Open May 15 to September 15.

Built in the 1880s to accommodate the cowboys and ranchers frequenting Medora, this two-story hotel still bears the brands burned

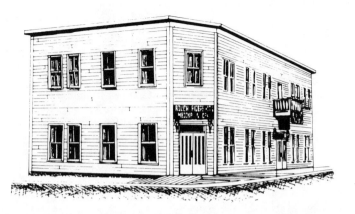

into its outside walls by exuberant cattlemen. The well-preserved, rough-sawed cedar building was one of the first restoration projects of the Gold Seal Company following its acquisition of much of the property in the old ghost town. When Teddy Roosevelt was in Medora as a young rancher in the Badlands, he would stay at the Rough Riders Hotel when he wasn't using his rooms above the town store. Most of the original furnishings survived intact through the seventy years that intervened between the building of the hotel and its restoration in the early 1960s. This furniture, carefully sandblasted, is in daily use at the hotel. Among the modern conveniences in the hotel's guest rooms, which otherwise retain an authentic old-West flavor, are wall-to-wall carpeting, air conditioning, modern bathrooms, and telephones. The building's unfinished horizontal cedar siding and simplicity of lines create an authentic Western setting that is free from commercialization.

The dining room at the Rough Riders offers a selection of beef that is appropriate to a hotel in a town that was founded to be a beef-packing center. Among the offerings are rib eye steak, tenderloin, barbecued back ribs, beef and shrimp kabob, and chopped buffalo steak. Roast buffalo and elk are available from time to time. Also on the menu are rainbow trout and lemon-baked chicken. All meals include salad, choice of vegetable or potato, and bread.

Accommodations: 9 rooms with private bath. *Driving Instructions:* Medora is about 30 miles west of Dickenson on I-94.

South Dakota

Canova, South Dakota

SKOGLUND FARM

Canova, SD 57321. 605-247-3445. *Innkeepers:* Alden and Delores Skoglund. Open all year.

The Skoglunds, a warm, friendly Midwestern farm family, have thrown open their doors to visitors wanting to escape to an honest-to-goodness working dairy farm. The farmhouse was built on the South Dakota prairie in 1910. It is an attractive white clapboard house with green shutters, a pillared porch, and a second-floor-balcony over the entrance to the house. Lawns and shade trees surround the home, and scattered about are the silver silos and red barns of the farmyard. The Skoglunds have about twenty milk cows as well as a collection of saddle horses, geese, turkeys, chickens, and even peacocks. Trixie, the house dog, presides over the farm, and Dolly, the pet pony, pulls guests around in a pony cart.

The farmhouse is a comfortable "down home" place where guests are just that—guests. The Skoglunds, Alden and Delores, make everyone feel right at home. All the rooms are comfortable, furnished with a blend of Midwestern Victorian, family treasures, a recliner, television, and a stereo.

Upstairs are the guest bedrooms, sharing the hall bathroom with its deep bathtub. The rooms have the same blend of Victorian antiques and family furniture as the rest of the house. The largest of the guest rooms has twin beds covered wth blue-and-white spreads and dust ruffles coordinated with the white-background wallpaper with blue flowers and the white-painted furniture.

Meals are served in the sunny dining room, where the windows offer views of the backyard, livestock, and barns. Breakfasts and dinners are served family style around the farm table. Delores will put up picnic lunches for guests who request them. The breakfasts and dinners here provide an excellent chance to sample hearty prairie farm meals. Everything is made from scratch, including the breads, pastries, and the main dishes. Much of the food is grown right on the farm: it has a productive garden where guests can help pick the evening's vegetables and salad greens in season. The farm's own hens provide the freshest of eggs.

The farm offers guests an opportunity to explore, watch, and help out with the farm chores, if they wish. The prairie land beyond the cattle pens is wilderness, the perfect place for a long stroll or a ride on one of the Skoglunds' horses. The creek out back is popular with rockhounds. Rockhound clubs have often come to the farm for a weekend, some fifteen strong, more than filling the five guest rooms; but it is that kind of place—a lot of fun for everyone, guests and innkeepers alike.

Accommodations: 5 rooms sharing hall bath. *Driving Instructions:* Exit I-90 at Salem. From the north edge of Salem go 8 miles north and 3 miles west. The farm is the first place on the north side.

Custer State Park, South Dakota

BLUE BELL LODGE AND RESORT

Custer State Park, Custer, SD 57730. 605-255-4531. *Innkeeper:* Phil Lampert. Open May 15 to October 1 and later if weather permits.

The Blue Bell Lodge is a fine old rustic lodge with log cabins scattered nearby in the seclusion of the ponderosa pines country of the mountainous Custer State Park. The lodge, at an elevation of 5,000 feet in the heart of the park's buffalo grounds, is owned by the state and leased on concession to Phil Lampert, a South Dakotan whose own living quarters are on the lodge's second floor.

The Blue Bell provides seventeen chinked-log cabins, eleven of which were built at the same time as the main lodge was, in 1920. The cabins are widely separated to ensure privacy. The older cabins are the smallest, have exposed-log walls inside, and contain heavy handmade pine furnishings in keeping with the atmosphere of a hunting lodge. Each has one room, housekeeping facilities, and heat. The cabins with kitchenettes do not come with dishes and utensils.

The main lodge is constructed inside and out of large ponderosa pine logs. The walls and 13-foot ceilings are of exposed chinked logs, and many animal trophies and stretched skins of local animals such as bison, elk, and deer are mounted on the walls. The building contains a lounging area for guests, a cocktail lounge, and a rough-log dining room warmed by a large stone fireplace with a log mantle. A trophy elk head peers down from the hearth wall amid many other mounted trophies. Lodge furnishings are of sturdy pine; the dining room is furnished with heavy pine captain's chairs and tables. One corner of the room is occupied by an authentic covered wagon, which adds a touch of the old frontier and doubles as a waitresses' station. The room is lit by the hearth fires and the lights in the wagonwheel chandeliers, part of the original décor.

Meals here are served family-style to both lodgers and the public. The dining room offers breakfast, lunch, and dinner; the cocktail lounge is open for before- and after-dinner drinks. The menu features Black Hills mountain trout, fresh from a local stream, and buffalo meat or roast beef. Home-baked pastries top off the meals.

A gift shop in the lodge offers gifts and craft objects—many, such as the Black Hills gold jewelry, are made locally of Black Hills materials. Innkeeper Phil Lampert specializes in buffalo trophies of all sorts, and he sells robes, skins, heads, and skulls in the shop. The lodge is centrally located in relation to most of the Black Hills attractions.

Accommodations: 17 cabins with private bath. *Driving Instructions:* The lodge is 42 miles south of Rapid City on Route 87, in the heart of Custer State Park. It is 12 miles from Custer and 25 miles from Hot Springs.

Custer State Park, the largest state park in the United States, occupies 128,000 acres of unspoiled natural beauty in the *Black Hills National Forest*. The park contains five crystal-clear lakes, mountain streams, rolling plains, high mountains including the jagged *Needles* formations to the north of the park, and the largest free-roaming herd of bison in the country, readily visible to tourists. Elk, antelope, and prairie dog are everywhere. Deer are so tame they come to cabins to be fed. Mountain trout can be caught in the well-stocked streams.

PALMER GULCH LODGE

Route 244, Hill City, South Dakota. *Mailing address:* P.O. Box 295C, Hill City, SD 57745. *605-574-2525. Innkeeper:* Al Johnson. Open May 1 through October 1.

The fifteen cabins at Palmer Gulch Lodge are scattered through more than 80 acres of meadow and trees in the center of the Black Hills at the foot of Harney Peak. Palmer Gulch has enjoyed a slow metamorphosis from its origins during the 1880 Gold Rush days, through becoming a golf course at the turn of the century, to the 1930s, when cabins were built (some more recently) and it began to function as a lodge and family resort. Palmer Creek trickles through the grounds and the Black Hills National Forest. Some of the cabins are log and some are frame; all have knotty pine walls and rustic pine furnishings. Fireplaces or wood-burning stoves provide their only source of heat, and many have porches and kitchenettes. The restaurant and lounge are in a large log building with picture windows, open beams, and a screened-porch dining area. A large fireplace and pine tables and chairs provide a rustic place to dine. The simple dinner menu features two steaks, chicken, shrimp, and fried fish. There is also a variety of sandwiches as well as a cold ham, turkey, and cheese plate.

Activities at the lodge center around the enjoyment of its scenic surroundings. Because it is a ranch lodge, there are a variety of horseback riding activities including breakfast trail-rides, trips to Harney Peak—the tallest peak east of the Rocky Mountains—and rides out to old mines, waterfalls, rock formations, and to Mount Rushmore. At the lodge are a heated swimming pool, hayrides, a playground for children, a games arcade, adult lounge, television lounge, and table games.

Accommodations: 15 rooms, all in cabins and all with private bath. *Driving Instructions:* Take Route 16 south from Rapid City to Mount Rushmore. Drive west of Mount Rushmore for 5 miles on Route 244.

Colorado

Boulder, Colorado

Boulder is the home of the University of Colorado and its more than 21,000 students. Many of Boulder's most important cultural attractions are on campus. Of note are the *Henderson Museum*, with its archaeological, anthropological, and natural-history exhibits, and *Fiske Planetarium*, with its particularly fine star-dome amphitheater. The *University Shakespeare Festival* is held at the Mary Rippon Outdoor Theatre every summer. The *Pioneer Museum* at 1655 Broadway contains early Western memorabilia. Both the *Bureau of Standards* and the *National Center for Atmospheric Research* have self-guided tours and displays relating to the scientific investigations carried out at the respective laboratories.

THE HOTEL BOULDERADO

2115 Thirteenth Street, Boulder, Colorado. Mailing address: P.O. Box 319, Boulder, CO 80306. 303-442-4344. *Innkeeper:* Jon Miller. Open all year.

The Hotel Boulderado, a historic landmark in Boulder, was for many years the tallest building around. Its five-story brick exterior has hardly changed since it first opened on New Year's Eve, 1908. The Boulderado was the first luxury hotel to be constructed in this city, and much of the original Victorian marble, glass, and woodwork remains. Over the years the ornate interior was allowed to deteriorate and was only recently saved by the present owners. The much-photographed lobby and mezzanine have undergone major renovation. The big glass dome over the lobby has had its stained glass replaced; the Victorian furnishings in both lobby and mezzanine were refinished, and appropriate period antiques were added. The grand staircase at one end of the marble-tiled room leads to the mezzanine and upstairs rooms and has original woodwork combining stained mahogany and cherry. Nightly entertainment in the mezzanine lounge includes concerts by local string quartets and brass chamber ensembles. The Boulderado contains two restaurants and three bars of its own and leases a third restaurant that offers Indian appetizers.

From the lobby, guest rooms may be reached by the oldest elevator in Colorado, built by the Otis Elevator Company in 1905. Rooms vary in size and décor; a few have been furnished in period antiques, but most have additional 1930s and 1940s hotel pieces. More than half have private baths. The hotel, the only one in downtown Boulder, is one block from the Boulder Mall with its many shops, cafés, night-clubs, and year-round activities. Rooms have full room-service menus, color television, and telephones.

Accommodations: 52 rooms, 31 with private bath. *Pets:* Not permitted. *Driving Instructions:* From Denver take U.S. 36 (the Boulder Freeway) to Boulder. Take Canyon Boulevard off Route 36 and drive to Thirteenth Street; turn right (north) and go three blocks to the corner of Thirteenth and Spruce streets.

Colorado Springs, Colorado

THE HEARTHSTONE INN

506 North Cascade Avenue, Colorado Springs, CO 80903. 303-473-4413. *Innkeepers:* Ruth Williams and Dorothy Williams. Open all year.

The Hearthstone Inn is a Queen Anne mansion in the Colorado Rockies. The elaborate gray-shingled exterior is trimmed in lavender, peach, plum, and bittersweet, all authentic Victorian colors. The mansion was built in 1885 by the Bemis family, who spared no expense in the detailing. For many years the hub of the city's social life, it fell into disrepair when the mines dried up and the wealthy residents left. In 1977, Dorothy Williams and Ruth Williams (not related) found the dilapidated estate. Before they knew it they had new careers as innkeepers and a very large, rundown house on their hands. They set about the task of complete and total authentic restoration, and they have succeeded splendidly. The house has been nominated for the National Register of Historic Places. Every piece of furniture and decoration in the inn has been carefully chosen, not a reproduction piece anywhere. Each room, hallway, and landing has its own special chosen wallpaper and décor. The quilts on each bed were made by a friend in Kansas, and the curtains, fashioned after Victorian styles, were made by Ruth's mother. Summers were spent scouring Midwest auctions and country sales for Victoriana; one very elaborate carved bedroom suite came from a pioneer family collection in California. The mansion is filled with cherry and walnut hand-carved beds, marble-top chests, authentic brass lighting fixtures, and pots of greenery.

The colors of the interior are more subdued than those of the façade. The parlor contains one of the four large fireplaces at the Hearthstone. It has a formal cherry mantelpiece and moss-green imported Italian tiles dating back to the mid-eighteenth century. The room is furnished with a pre-Civil War couch of hand-carved woods, cushioned in crushed burgundy velvet; a matching set of chairs; a burnt-orange carpet; and curtains with deep burgundy velvet swags on the three tall windows. Guests enjoy gathering around the piano for an evening singalong or relaxing by the fire.

The Hearthstone offers guests a choice of fifteen bedrooms. It would be difficult to pick a favorite here; each has its own special feature and name. The ground floor has the Garden Room overlooking a shady garden; the Pantry, a corner room looking out on Pikes Peak; and the Victorian Suite (the inn's only suite), with a library, an ornate working fireplace, a window nook, handsome, high Victorian beds, and an adjoining bedroom with two twin brass beds. The second-floor rooms are bright and sunny with views of the Rockies and the inn's gardens. The Library is the only other guest room with a working fireplace. The third floor offers four rooms with slanting ceilings and Victorian wallpapers. All the rooms have oak, walnut, or cherry beds and dressers, marble-top tables, and washstands with the original china bowls and pitchers. The beds are covered with antique coverlets and handmade quilts. The Solarium on the second floor, the favorite of honeymooners, has a secluded little porch off the room with views of the mountains framed by latticework.

Mornings in the Hearthstone are a treat. Breakfasts, included in room rates, are served in the sunny dining room warmed by fires in the fireplace. Dorothy and Ruth cook meals not often found in inns, with a different menu every day. One morning it might be fresh fruits, hot orange bread, and a breakfast cheese pie of ricotta; on another, sticky buns and baked apples or a variety of quiches and soufflés. Their creamed chicken on home-baked buns would get the laziest person in the world out of bed. Hot coffee and tea are always available. The inn is on a large corner lot with gardens and ash and elm trees. The colors of the house are reflected in the old-fashioned flower gardens in front and in the ever changing hues of the distant mountains.

Accommodations: 15 rooms, most with private bath. *Pets:* Permitted only in the Pantry Room, which has access to the back door. *Driving Instructions:* I-25, exit 143 (Uintah Street) east away from the mountains to the third light (three long blocks). Turn right on Cascade Avenue and go seven blocks to the inn on the corner of Cascade and St. Vrain.

SOWARD RANCH

P.O. Box 130, Creede, CO 81130. 303-658-2295 May 1 to November 1; otherwise 303-658-2228. *Innkeepers:* Margaret and Howard Lamb. Open late May to mid-October.

The Soward Ranch, by the Rio Grande, has been in the same family for a hundred years. Its original section was homesteaded in 1886 by Ellen and Dan Soward, who arrived in the area in 1879 and operated a stagecoach stop and the post office. The Soward's daughter, Mrs. Emma McCrone, still helps out at the ranch and has many colorful tales to tell of the old days. Three generations work together at the ranch today: Mrs. McCrone, Howard and Margaret Lamb, and their sons Jim, Scott, and Steve, who hope to continue the operation in future years. The Lambs' daughter Susan and her husband, Fred, are the innkeepers of a fine little country inn in northern Vermont, the Mountain View in Waitsfield.

In 1932, rustic cabins were added over the ranch property; each was assured privacy by its location. The cabins come with full bath, heat, and cooking and refrigeration facilities. Dishes, utensils, bedding, linen, and towels are supplied. Most cabins are fully modernized, but two pioneer cabins are favored by guests who prefer roughing it. Three have fireplaces and one a Franklin stove. At this time the Lambs do not rent horses, offer food, or sell supplies, but it is a pleasant jaunt into Creede for provisions. The Lambs' son Jim runs the Old Miner's Inn restaurant in Creede, which is open daily for lunch and dinner.

Soward Ranch, in a scenic open valley at 9,000 feet, is surrounded by mountains, outstanding views, and fresh air. Trout fishing is the main recreation here, and it is excellent. The best fishing spots include several miles along the Red Mountain Trout and Lime Creeks; in three small private lakes with moderately good fishing; and—for the accomplished fisherman a real challenge—the Rio Grande. Mainly, however, Soward Ranch is for relaxing in an unspoiled setting.

Accommodations: 12 housekeeping cabins with bath. *Pets:* Not permitted. *Driving Instructions:* The ranch is 14 miles southwest of Creede. Drive 7 miles on asphalt road (Route 149), then turn at Middle Creek Road, which has a gravel surface, and continue 7 miles.

Cripple Creek, Colorado

IMPERIAL HOTEL

123 North Third Street, Cripple Creek, CO 80813. 303-689-2713.
Innkeepers: Wayne and Dorothy Mackin. Open mid-May to mid-October.

The Imperial is the last of the old Cripple Creek hotels to have survived from the boom period before the turn of the century. The hotel was constructed in 1896 by Mrs. E. F. Collins. In its heyday it was the queen of the town, a base for the wining and dining of financiers, geologists, mining engineers, and their clients from the East Coast who assembled in Cripple Creek ready to make their fortunes in the newly discovered gold. Unlike most mining town hotels built during the boom, the Imperial never closed its doors except for a brief period during World War II.

When the Mackins bought the three-story brick hotel in 1946, it was in sad neglect and had no functioning kitchen, having served as a boarding house since 1925. Most people in the town felt that the hotel could not be run as a profitable enterprise, but the Mackins persisted. Room by room they refurbished the place, installing furnishings rescued from the even older Antlers Hotel in Colorado Springs and a backbar from a local pool hall. They hired local high school girls as waitresses, and Mrs. Mackin's mother joined the staff as pastry cook and hostess. The hotel gained a spreading reputation for good food and hospitality. Early on, it made the fortunate decision to invite the Piper Players, a struggling group of actors and actresses, to set up headquarters at the Imperial. The group was signed to present a season of old-time melodramas. The 1948 summer season saw attendance by 4,800, and the theater is now considered to be the foremost exponent of melodrama in the country, presenting only carefully researched plays that are authentic, dating from the 1840 to 1900 period. More than 800,000 people have attended performances. *Time* magazine said of the Imperial Players: "Most melodrama groups are influenced by the quality of the Imperial Players, the 'Old Vic' of modern melodrama." The theater season is from early June through Labor Day.

The Imperial, a classic Victorian hotel, offers thirty guest rooms (plus a modern motel unit). Those wishing a more old-fashioned room furnished with antiques should request one when making their reservations. Guest rooms and public rooms have carefully selected period wallpapers. Many of the furnishings, including the period lighting pieces, have been rescued from historic Colorado buildings slated for demolition. Recently, for example, the Mackins saved the front desk and box-office cage from the old First National Bank of Colorado Springs. Stained-glass doors in the dining room as well as leaded and stained-glass panels over the entrance doors were salvaged from the razing of Glockner Hospital and Sanitarium in Colorado Springs. The Red Rooster lounge has a small bar that once served miners in the Red Rooster Saloon near Twin Lakes, Colorado.

The dining rooms at the Imperial are set with white or gold linen and a variety of furniture of several vintages. The restaurant serves a luncheon buffet and repeats the buffet in the evening on a more elaborate scale, always featuring roast baron of beef. There are two other entrées available each night for those who prefer not to partake of the buffet.

Accommodations: 30 rooms, 16 with private bath. *Pets:* Not permitted. *Driving Instructions:* Cripple Creek may be reached by means of Route 67 the year round or by means of the very scenic Gold Camp Road, an improved gravel road, in the summer only.

Cripple Creek is a town of 750 people that lies over the mountains from Colorado Springs. A paved highway system connects Colorado Springs to Cripple Creek, skirting Pikes Peak. However, during the summer months, tourists who are wiling to brave the gravel-surfaced Gold Camp Road may drive directly to Cripple Creek through scenery so breathtaking that it prompted Theodore Roosevelt to call the journey "the trip that bankrupts the English language." From the top of Tenderfoot Hills, visitors may enjoy a view of the Sangre de Cristo mountains that ring the town of Cripple Creek. For those who do not attempt the gravel road to the high country, the *Cripple Creek and Victor Narrow Gauge Railroad* is a pleasant alternative. Passengers can enjoy views from open cars that pass historic cabins, gold mines, and trestles on the way to Anaconda, an abandoned mining camp. The train, pulled by a coal-burning locomotive, operates daily from June 1 through the first week in October with departures every forty-five minutes from 10 to 5.

THE BALLOON RANCH

Southwest of La Garita, Colorado. Mailing address: Star Route, P.O. Box 41, Del Norte, CO 81132. 303-754-2533. *Innkeeper:* David Levin. Open Memorial Day through Thanksgiving.

The site of the Balloon Ranch, the San Luis Valley, was chosen because of its open spaces and beauty. The ranch's 200 acres are in one of America's biggest mountain valleys, at 8,000 feet, surrounded by the Rio Grande National Forest, the Great Sand Dunes, mountain peaks, and mountain streams. The ranch is a resort catering primarily to aspiring balloonists but equally appealing to people interested in a wide range of outdoor activities. Rafting on the Rio Grande, technical rock climbing, dune buggying, horseback riding, hiking, fishing, tennis, and swimming are available. The Balloon Ranch, not just for the athlete, also accommodates those lazy souls who want to loll about and enjoy the scenery.

The modern main lodge building blends with its desert landscape. The interior is spacious, with high-beamed ceilings, a big stone fireplace, and hand-crafted furnishings. The white expanse of walls is accented here and there with balloon art and Indian rugs and crafts. The main dining room is in the lodge, where guests are served meals ranchstyle at long tables. After dinner, guests often congregate around the fire in the lounge and recount the day's adventures.

The Balloon Ranch has a variety of accommodations. In the lodge are rooms ranging from singles to a bunk room sleeping three or four. The ranch also has cabins with the same range of room sizes. There is also a new deluxe and secluded cabin.

The ranch offers balloon rides of approximately one hour. They also have an introductory course, flight training, and a complete certification course (twelve hours of flight instruction and ground school). Real ballooning enthusiasts can purchase a balloon here, and the ranch will throw in free instruction. The Balloon Ranch site was chosen for its excellent ballooning properties: perfect observation, chase, and recovery as well as predictable weather conditions.

Introductory technical mountain climbing classes are also available here, taught by qualified professional mountain climbers. Technical climbing equipment is included in the price of a day's instruction. The ranch has four-wheel-drive tours, rafting tips, and field biologist guides to point out the many varieties of animal life in the area. The innkeeper, David Levin, and his staff obviously love their ballooning ranch, and with good reason. It is an unusual and exciting place.

Accommodations: 12 rooms, 4 with private bath. *Pets:* Not permitted. *Driving Instructions:* The ranch is 10 miles north of Del Norte. From Del Norte take Route 112 northeast 3 miles to the La Garita turnoff. Then go north 7 miles and turn left at the Balloon Ranch sign and go 1 mile. From the north, go 17½ miles south of Saguache to La Garita and the Balloon Ranch turnoff.

Del Norte is in the San Luis Valley, surrounded on three sides by the vast *Rio Grande National Forest.* The National Forest contains 1.8 million acres of unbelievable beauty. The town is on the banks of the world-famous *Rio Grande.* One exciting way to see the river and the scenic country along its banks is by raft. In South Fork to the west on the Rio Grande, the *Spruce Ski Lodge* has two- to four-hour trips on the river from May to September. Call 303-837-9980. *Wolf Creek Ski Area,* 18 miles southwest of South Fork in the Rio Grande National Forest, is off Route 160 and has powder skiing and large amounts of snow from November to mid-April. Northeast of Del Norte is the *Great Sand Dunes National Monument,* 57 square miles of shifting, wind-shaped dunes, the highest in the United States. They are at the edge of the San Luis Valley and parallel to the towering *Sangre de Cristo Mountains,* whose peaks reach above 14,000 feet. The dunes sweep right up to the base of the rugged mountains, creating an eerie contrast. Alamosa is at the south gateway to the huge National Park.

Durango, a historic mining town in the San Juan Mountains of southwestern Colorado, is on the famed old Navajo Trail, which traverses the rugged mountain lands and the areas explored by the Spanish conquistadors. Crossing the Navajo Trail in Durango is the Million Dollar Highway, Route 550, named for the large amounts of gold that pass along it. Durango is the largest and most tourist-oriented of the mountain mining towns. One of its centers of activity is the Strater Hotel, with its old-fashioned *Diamond Circle Theater* and *Diamond Circle Arcade* shopping area. A few blocks from the hotel is the *Durango and Rio Grande Depot*, home station for the historic *Denver and Rio Grande Railroad*—a narrow-gauge gold train that runs on a 100-mile round trip between Durango and the historic town *Silverton*.

GENERAL PALMER HOUSE

567 Main Street, Durango, CO 81301. 303-247-4747. *Innkeeper:* Susan Williams. Open all year.

The General Palmer House, built in 1898, was named after General Jackson Palmer, the founder of the Denver and Rio Grande Railroad. The hotel was fully renovated and remodeled in 1964. Today, the flavor of the hotel is reminiscent of the earlier era, but most of the guest rooms have been modernized and contain modern furnishings. Five of the guest rooms have reproduction antique furniture and are called the "Executive" rooms. Each guest room has a private shower and bath as well as telephones and color television. (Some of the rooms are in an annex across the parking lot from the original hotel.) The lobby retains its original paneled wainscotting with wallpaper above. It also has brass and Tiffany-style chandeliers and wall sconces. The lobby is the only hotel room on the first floor; the remaining space is rented to other Durango businesses. No meals are served at the hotel, but the Strater Hotel and the Palace Restaurant, adjacent to the Narrow Gauge Depot, have popular public dining rooms.

Accommodations: 35 rooms with private bath. *Pets:* Not permitted. *Driving Instructions:* Durango is at the intersection of Routes 550 and 160 in southwestern Colorado. The hotel is on Main Street.

STRATER HOTEL

699 Main Avenue, Durango, Colorado. Mailing address: P.O. Drawer E, Durango, CO 81301. 303-247-4431. *Innkeeper:* James Blomstrom. Open all year.

The Strater is a grand old Victorian hotel. It has been in continuous operation since 1887, when twenty-year-old Henry Strater undertook the task and considerable gamble of building the large luxury hotel in the frontier mining town of Durango. The Strater was leased to a Mr. Rice. After a series of misunderstandings, Mr. Strater spitefully built another hotel, the Columbian, adjoining the original. Eventually both hotels ended up under the ownership of the Barker family, proprietors since 1926. The present owner is Earl Barker.

The Strater has been meticulously restored and maintained. Many modern conveniences have been slipped into the Victorian guest rooms, all of which are fully air-conditioned and have phones and television. Sixty-seven are completely furnished with the ornate furniture and décor of the turn of the century. The Victorian rooms have some of the fanciest walnut high-backed beds to be found anywhere. One features a ceiling-high canopy of carved burled hardwood and a tufted deep-purple velvet lining, accompanying marble-top dressers, velvet cushioned sofas and chairs, heavy cream-colored bedspreads, and velvet drapes. Walls are covered in various ways, some with white paint, others with flocked-gold and burgundy wallpapers, and some have exposed bricks and wood paneling. Ornate gilt frames containing old photographs, prints, and oils decorate the halls and rooms throughout. All rooms have private baths, some very modern and others outfitted with claw-footed tubs.

The Strater is in the restored historic district of Durango, its sidewalks lit by old gas lanterns. Inside the brick four-story hotel, the lobby, two dining rooms, a saloon, and a 300-seat theater are decked out in Victorian antiques, etched and stained-glass windows, Tiffany-style chandeliers, paintings, and velvets and satins.

The two restaurants, the Opera House and the Columbian Room, offer meals in very different atmospheres. The Columbian Room is formal and dignified, with gold-trimmed mirrors and brass candelabras set on marble-top walnut sideboards. The more casual and old-time Opera House has Tiffany shades and stained-glass windows. In summer the staff entertains guests with light opera and Broadway tunes. Metropolitan and European opera star Edith Mason's antique mirrored buffet is the focal point of the restaurant. Both dining rooms feature a fine selection of entrées, such as Rocky Mountain trout sautéed in butter and lemon juice, tenderloin on toasted French bread with Madeira sauce and a garnish of melon, or an Oriental chicken dish with julienne vegetables and cashews served over rice. There are also thick steaks and the most reasonable prices around.

Diamond Belle Saloon is a popular place with its "Gay Nineties" décor, a honky-tonk piano, and bartenders and cancan girls all in authentic costume. The Diamond Circle Theater, open in the summer months, presents "turn of the century" plays and vaudeville acts with an "olio"—an intermission performance of banjo and piano playing while actors serve drinks.

Accommodations: 94 rooms with private bath. *Pets:* Only small trained pets are allowed. *Driving Instructions:* Durango is in the far southwest corner of the state, where Route 550, the famous Million Dollar Highway over the mountains, crosses over the Navajo Trail, Route 160, also known as the "Western Wonderway."

THE PECK HOUSE

83 Sunny Avenue, Empire, Colorado. Mailing address: Box 428, Empire, CO 80438. 303-569-9870. Open all year.

The Peck House is the oldest hotel in Colorado still in operation. Built as the family home of James Peck in 1860, the wood-frame building was initially a four-room house. Peck, a wealthy and adventurous Chicago merchant, was lured west in 1859 by the challenge of the frontier and the chance to find gold. In 1872, he converted his home to the Peck House to accommodate visiting mining executives. Running water was provided by burning lengths of aspen hollow with a hot poker and then fitting them together and running the wooden pipe to a spring to the north of the house. The Peck House had the first electric lights in the area, thanks to power generated by its water wheel. For many years before the automobile, the Peck House was a stop for the stagecoaches running over Berthoud Pass. Over the years, the house was added onto in several directions, and today a long front porch overlooks the valley that first attracted Peck to the area. The present kitchen, bar, and reception area are located within the original building. Much of the furniture dates back to the time of the original owners. Over the years, the Peck House has entertained such luminaries as Generals Grenville Dodge and William Tecumseh Sherman and showman Phineas T. Barnum.

The downstairs portion of the Peck House is primarily devoted to the public rooms. There are two sitting rooms as well as a lounge, a bar, and a dining room. The larger of the sitting rooms has a comfortable arrangement of Victorian furniture including two easy chairs, a pair of rockers, and a bookcase crammed with books available for guests' reading. This room has the feeling of the front parlor of many homes of the Victorian era. The dining room has red carpeting and white walls on which are hung nineteenth-century prints and photographs of the area. The windows have red velvet curtains, and the tables are set with red linen tablecloths and fresh flowers. The intimate room has twelve tables, and a fire frequently burns in its fireplace.

The dinner menu's five starters include French onion soup, sautéed mushrooms, steamed clams, escargots, and shrimp served in

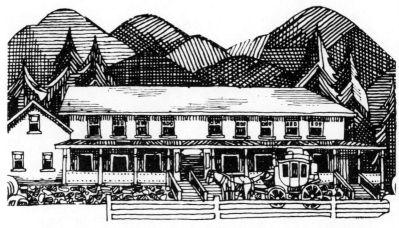

their shells with a lemon sauce. Entrées, accompanied by a soup of the day and a spinach or dinner salad plus bread and rice or potato, range from steaks and roasts to poultry to several seafood selections. The scallops poached in wine sauce and topped with sliced water chestnuts and the poached Icelandic codfish with parsley sauce are the least commonly encountered of the entrée selections.

Of the eleven guest rooms at the Peck House, the only one on the first-floor is furnished in a blend of Victorian and "old West" furniture that includes a pair of dressers and a double bedstead—all made of bird's-eye maple. The bed is flanked by a pair of matching side stands with marble tops, which have brass chimney lamps on them. A Victorian bowl and pitcher set on a table in the room add to the period feeling. A window in this room overlooks the same scene as those in the bar, and red velvet drapes are swagged on it and hang from wooden rings on a wooden window pole. A door opens onto the front porch directly from this room. The bridal suite is the best room upstairs. Probably the original bridal suite, it has two windows facing Union Pass and a third that catches the morning sun. It has an iron double bed with a mahogany table on each side topped with an antique globe lamp. An elaborate walnut dresser with swinging mirror and a cane-seat maple rocker complete the room.

Accommodations: 11 rooms, 5 with private bath. *Pets:* Not permitted. *Driving Instructions:* Take I-70 to the Empire-Granby exit. The inn is in the center of the town of Empire.

Green Mountain Falls, Colorado

OUTLOOK LODGE

P.O. Box 5, Green Mountain Falls, CO 80819. 303-684-2303. *Innkeepers:* The Ahern family. Open June through Labor Day.

Outlook Lodge is an old "country Victorian" tucked away in the secluded mountain village of Green Mountain Falls at the foot of Pikes Peak. The lodge is a Victorian parsonage built during the Colorado Gold Rush days of the late nineteenth century. In those days the town was a booming tourist mecca with five big hotels on the shores of the stream-fed lake. Outlook Lodge carries on the traditions of warm Western hospitality from the late nineteenth century. The Aherns, while looking for a mountain cabin for family vacations, fell in love with the lodge amid tall pine trees with a little mountain creek running through its property. The building came with stained-glass and big bay windows, spacious dining room, large, comfortable parlor, and most of the original Victorian furnishings. There was even a walk-in pantry. The temptation to buy was irresistible, and the Aherns found themselves running a very popular and successful guest house. The Aherns, freelance writers and teachers, entered wholeheartedly into this new venture.

Lodge rooms are either wood-paneled or papered with floral patterns. Breakfasts are served family-style around the long table in the antique-filled dining room. Freshly baked sweet rolls and carrot, corn, and banana breads come hot from the oven and are served with pots of jams and jellies and fresh creamery butter. The coffee pot is always ready with steaming-hot brew. The parlor is warmed by a tiled fireplace, and guests are welcome to relax and visit in this room with its plants and old rockers.

The staircase leading to the guest rooms looks like something out of "Goldilocks and the Three Bears"—carved and woodsy. The guest rooms with their spool beds and other period Victorian bedroom furniture blend with the puffy quilts and braided rag rugs to create an atmosphere of old-fashioned comfort. If you remember to leave your boots outside your door before you retire, they will be waiting polished for you the next morning. Another Ahern special treat is a hot cup of coffee in bed in the morning if you wish, though it's much more fun to join the family for breakfast in the dining room or take

your cup out onto the gingerbready veranda overlooking the alpine village of Green Mountain Falls.

The lodge is ideally situated one block from the lake, a swimming pool, and the town with its restaurants. There is no lack of entertainment in the area. The town has a stable with horses for hire and tennis courts. Hiking is excellent in the surrounding hills. The Rocky Mountain lakes and streams offer good fishing. Mountain-cool evenings around the lodge's fireplace, a community sing at the old piano, and mornings at the breakfast table with all its muffins and breads make Outlook Lodge the perfect home base for a Colorado vacation. The family atmosphere of this house encourages lasting friendships among guests and their hosts.

Accommodations: 12 rooms, 4 with private bath. *Driving Instructions:* Green Mountain Falls is 15 miles east of Colorado Springs on Route 24.

Ouray, Colorado

BAKER'S MANOR GUEST HOUSE

317 Second Street, Ouray, CO 81427. 303-325-4574. *Innkeepers:* John and Nancy Nixon. Open June through September.

Ouray is a valley village surrounded by the San Juan mountains. Baker's Manor is a pleasant alternative to the area motels as a base to enjoy a region that (like many others in the Rockies) has dubbed itself the "Switzerland of America." As you enter the canyon from the surrounding mountains, you will certainly agree that the Ouray region is a top contender for the title. At an altitude of 7,800 feet, Baker's Manor is one of the loftiest inns we have listed. The two-story home, built in 1881, now contains a private residence on the first floor with the guest rooms on the second floor. Most of the guest rooms have antique beds and dressers and are a true travel bargain.

Accommodations: 6 rooms sharing a bath and shower. *Pets:* Not permitted. *Driving Instructions:* Take Route 550 to the center of Ouray. The guest house is one block west of Main Street between Third and Fourth avenues.

HOTEL ST. ELMO

P.O. Box 1850, Ouray, CO 81427. 303-325-4318. *Innkeepers:* Chuck Norton and Richard and Cyndee Miers. Open all year.

In 1899, Kitty Hiatt, a lady of questionable background, built the Hotel St. Elmo to augment her successful Bon-Ton restaurant. The hotel has been in continuous operation ever since, first serving miners, then the travelers who slowly became a source of income to the town as the mining efforts declined. Many of the other fine hotels in Ouray did not survive the decades, succumbing to fire or neglect. The St. Elmo, however, is a sturdy brick two-story building heavily influenced by the art nouveau style rather than the strictly Victorian movement popular at the time. The hotel has a large, old-fashioned lobby frequented by guests who gather there for coffee or tea. Most of the original furnishings have survived, an advantage peculiar to hotels that have remained in continuous use. The owners have also sought out additional pieces to supplement the original ones. The guest rooms are generally large.

The Bon-Ton Restaurant lives on at the St. Elmo, though it offers a different menu from Miss Kitty's days. Today's is brief and allows the chef to concentrate on preparing a few dishes well. It is Italian in derivation, except for three steak items and a seafood special, usually crepes. Three appetizers head the menu: a spinach-cheese crepe, an antipasto called Propasto Circus Maximus, and quiche Lorraine. Minestrone soup is also available as a starter. Entrées include spaghetti prepared three ways, ravioli, fettucini, veal parmesan, and several others. Dessert might include pecan pie and cheese cake.

Accommodations: 24 rooms, 18 with private bath. *Pets:* Not permitted. *Driving Instructions:* Take Route 550 to the center of Ouray and the hotel.

Ouray, in the heart of the San Juan Mountains, was named for the celebrated Ute Indian chief who died in 1880. Founded in 1875, Ouray was a gold and silver mining town of more than 2,000 residents. It was incorporated in 1876 and soon had richly productive gold and copper mines. Today, the Idarado Mine, near Red Mountain Pass, is the second largest in the state and the leader in the production of copper ore. Ouray has a population of 800 and is about 7,800 feet above sea level. The town has a number of historic houses and public buildings that may be seen in a short walking tour of Ouray following a guide available at the *Ouray County Historical Museum*. The museum, in the former St. Joseph's Hospital built in 1885, is open daily 10:30 to 4:00 from May 30 to mid-September. A modern swimming facility at the *Ouray Municipal Bathhouse* has the largest pool in southwestern Colorado and is filled with water from the local mineral hot springs. There are several area ghost towns and almost endless scenic vistas. The area waterfalls are striking, especially the 285-foot drop at Box Canyon. The Chamber of Commerce, P.O. Box 145, Ouray, CO 81427, will be happy to send more information. Their telephone number is 303-325-4746.

Redstone, Colorado

THE HISTORIC REDSTONE INN

0082 Redstone Boulevard, Redstone, CO 81623. 303-963-2526.
Innkeeper: Anne Van Dis. Open all year.

The Redstone Inn represents but a fraction of the real estate holdings developed in the area by the industrialist and coal baron John Cleveland Osgood. He constructed the inn in 1902 to provide housing for his bachelor miners working the local coal mines and for the many guests he attracted to the area but did not wish to entertain at his neighboring Cleveholm Manor. The inn is a copy of a Dutch tavern with its clock tower rising from one corner of the U-shaped, three-story, half-timbered building. A distinctive feature is the series of balconies surrounding each floor on all sides. The latest addition to the 1902 structure was provided by Frank E. Kistler of the Hotel Coronado, who bought the inn in the 1950s and added a wing. Kistler had planned to develop Redstone into a giant Colorado resort, with the Redstone Inn as its focal point, but he died when the plan was barely begun.

Today, the inn is divided into two lodging sections. The new section, started by Kistler, has semi-Western-style rooms. They are quite large, with two double beds in each. All but four open onto the second-floor balcony and have views of the town of Redstone and the surrounding mountains. The older section has smaller rooms with old-fashioned wallpaper, brass or iron beds, and much of the hand-pegged miner's furniture that was originally in the inn.

The inn's public rooms include an elegant dining room with a fireplace and two parlors with fireplaces. Throughout the premises is the Osgood collection of antique paintings, tapestries, and furniture. The inn's distinctly European feeling is enhanced by its rural setting.

The Redstone serves breakfast, lunch, and dinner Monday through Saturday and both breakfast and a buffet on Sunday. All meals in its restaurant are served to guests and the public. Appetizers include an unusual cranberry and sweet potato quiche, tempura mushrooms, a relish plate of the day, and a choice of soups. Entrées include salmon steak, trout, coquilles Saint-Jacques, a fancy seafood salad, honey and cardamom chicken, and three cuts of steak. So renowned is the baked Alaska that dinner guests have been known to drive there just for that dish.

For summer activities the inn has a tennis court and a glass-enclosed swimming pool. Riding is offered at the Redstone's stables with guided trail rides available. In winter there is a complete cross-country skiing center, which offers guided trail rides. Also available in the winter is instruction in ice climbing and wilderness photography. Aspen is but an hour's drive from the inn.

Accommodations: 26 rooms, 25 with private bath. *Pets:* Permitted in lower level rooms only. *Driving Instructions:* From Denver, take I-70 to Glenwood Springs, turn west onto Route 82 to Carbondale, then take Route 133 south to Redstone.

Silverton, Colorado

GRAND IMPERIAL HOTEL

1219 Greene Street, Silverton, Colorado. Mailing address: P.O. Box 97, Silverton, CO 81433. 303-387-5527. *Innkeeper:* Michael Ludwig. Open all year.

The Grand Imperial is a brick-and-stone Victorian hotel built in 1882 by an Englishman to serve the newly opened narrow-gauge railroad. The Denver and Rio Grande Railroad connected the many mines of Silverton with the smelters at Durango. Today, the line is run as a tourist attraction. Stones for the sides of the hotel were gathered locally, and the bricks were made especially at local brick kilns. Plans for this hotel were made well in advance of its actual construction. The best witness to this is the cherry back bar that survives today in the lounge. It is more than 35 feet long and was constructed especially for the Grand Imperial in 1879, three years before the hotel opened its doors. It was then shipped around Cape Horn to San Francisco, where it was put on several covered wagons and sent over the rugged trails to Silverton. It has stood in the same spot for about a century.

Michael Ludwig recently purchased the hotel and began a large-scale two-year restoration project. He has been careful to maintain the Victorian atmosphere throughout the hotel. The guest rooms are mostly decorated with period antiques that include brass and iron beds and accessory pieces from the same period. The dining room has a second bar that was recently installed as a showpiece, having spent many decades in a variety of taverns throughout Silverton. Another distinctive feature of the dining room is its black walnut tables, unique in the locale. There are several mementos of past gambling at the Grand Imperial, including a handsome antique roulette table and several old slot machines. The innkeeper is proud of a sailing ship carved by Joseph Imhoff around the turn of the century and given to the hotel in its youth. Imhoff was a noted painter as well as a wood-carver; his portrait of Lillian Russell hangs at the head of the stairs. An interesting touch in the lounge is the L-shaped balcony overlooking the room. A fireplace here is used in cool weather.

The dining room at the Grand Imperial serves a selection of American cooking with the emphasis on simple fare of the meat-and-potatoes variety. There are steaks, quail, trout, lobster, and shrimp dishes

—all accompanied by home-baked breads, rolls, and pastries. The loung features live entertainment daily in summer and on special weekends in winter. The latest attraction at the hotel is Michael Ludwig's special ski packages. This area is an excellent spot for all kinds of winter sports, and the Grand Imperial offers skiers package deals with all-day lift tickets and transportation to and from Purgatory Ski Area nearby.

Accommodations: 40 rooms with private bath. *Pets:* Inquire in advance. *Driving Instructions:* Route 550 runs directly into Silverton and becomes Greene Street.

Telluride, Colorado

NEW SHERIDAN HOTEL AND BAR

231 West Colorado Avenue, Telluride, Colorado. Mailing address: P.O. Box 980, Telluride, CO 81435. 303-728-4351. *Innkeeper:* Walter C. McClennan. Open all year.

The New Sheridan, a three-story brick hotel, was built in 1895 and 1899. The handsome Victorian structure was the pride of Telluride in its youth and offered, for many years, the finest food and lodging in the area. As the mining era that had caused Telluride to flourish at the turn of the century began to wane, so did the fortunes of the New

Sheridan. Then, in 1977, an Ohio developer and renovator of historic buildings, Walter C. McClellan, bought the old building.

Today, the New Sheridan is a fully modern hotel that has been restored and renovated to retain its Victorian ambience while incorporating such modern conveniences as private bathrooms. Each of its bedrooms has brass beds, oak furniture, and stained-glass lighting fixtures. On the first floor is an authentic Victorian bar and lounge, the centerpiece of which is the long cherrywood bar that was imported for the New Sheridan from Austria when the hotel opened in the 1890s. The bar was used in several scenes of a 20th Century-Fox movie about Butch Cassidy and the Sundance Kid. Also on this floor is Charley's Chinese Restaurant. Among the specialties served in this room, heavy with the scarlet décor of the early 1900s, are General Tsao Chicken, Szechwan Duckling, Charley's Special Shrimp, and Szechwan Whole Crispy Fish. The initial plans for the restaurant had called for a French-Continental menu, but there are so many excellent restaurants in town, including a French one, that the decision was made to bring in a highly respected Chinese chef. The result has been a runaway success for the restaurant, especially among the winter ski crowd. The bar's rear wall is a stained-glass partition that separates the bar from a smaller room often used for backgammon. Outside the hotel is a landscaped patio called the Sheridan Garden, which is used for lunch and cocktails during the summer months. Although not actually part of the hotel, immediately next door are a coed sauna and a Jacuzzi, both available to guests of the hotel.

Accommodations: 30 rooms, 9 with private bath. *Pets:* Not permitted. *Driving Instructions:* Take Colorado 145 directly into Telluride.

Dizzy Gillespie is quoted as saying: "If Telluride ain't paradise, then heaven can wait." Whatever Telluride is, it certainly is having a renaissance following many years of financial depression that ensued after billions of dollars in precious minerals were wrenched from its many miles of mining tunnels. Telluride's new mother lode is the skiing boom. Surrounded by the 14,000-foot peaks of the San Juan mountains, the Telluride Ski Area dominates the local downhill action. The Plunge is the steepest and one of the longest ski runs in North America, descending over a vertical drop of 3,200 feet.

Idaho

Mountain Home, Idaho

LA-PAT HOTEL

195 N2W, Mountain Home, ID 83647. 208-587-9950. *Innkeeper:* Melvin and Gladys Freeman. Open all year.

The La-Pat Hotel is a purposefully old-fashioned, in-town hostelry across from the Union Pacific Amtrak Station. At the turn of the century there was widespread immigration to Idaho and Nevada by Basque sheepherders. The La-Pat was built by a Basque gentleman who used the building to house his herders during the winter months. In its early days, Basque food was served at the hotel and Basque dances were frequently held there.

The Basque community has since moved on, but the Freemans have preserved the atmosphere of the early 1900s. The guest rooms retain their original high ceilings, and each has the early iron beds, now painted gold, with new box springs and mattresses. Bedspreads and matching drapes of a patchwork design, and glass hurricane lamps with floral designs are on the tables. There are also period mahogany chests and rockers. The hotel's large lobby has an old Grafanola record player, complete with hand crank. The television

lounge's pot-bellied stove offers a warm fire on chilly evenings. The lounge is decorated with wallpaper that depicts events of the American Revolution. Typical of the period, most bath and lavatory facilities are in the hall. Each of the four hall bathrooms has its original claw-foot tub. No food is served at the hotel.

Accommodations: 24 rooms, 2 with private bath, the rest sharing 4 hall baths and 4 hall restrooms. *Pets:* Not permitted. *Driving Instructions:* Take exit 95 (Mountain Home) from I-80.

INDIAN CREEK GUEST RANCH

Route 2, Box 105, North Fork, ID 83466. *Telephone:* Dial "O" and ask for the Salmon, Idaho, operator. Ask her for the Indian Creek Guest Ranch at 24F 211. *Innkeepers:* Jack and Lois Briggs. Open May 1 to November 1.

Indian Creek offers truly remote, rustic vacationing. The ranch consists of a main lodge and four guests cabins scattered on the property, which is ringed by rough stone walls. Mountain slopes rise abruptly from behind the cabins, and the smell of a pine fire in the fireplace greets you on arrival. If you are heading to Indian Creek, plan to put behind you your dependence on some of the refinements of civilization. There is no electricity here, only propane-powered gas lamps. However, each cabin has its own hot and cold running water and private bathroom. The lone radio-telephone in the lodge is run by battery power, so don't plan to conduct long-distance business conference from the ranch.

The main lodge was known as the Red Onion Bar in the 1890s and early twentieth century, when the stagecoach went through the property and on out to Ulysses, now a ghost town. The lodge borders on the Idaho wilderness and has a screened-in dining room looking out over the mountains. It serves simple, home-cooked foods such as prime ribs, steaks, chicken, spaghetti, barbecued ribs, hot rolls, biscuits, and muffins. The fishing for trout is good in the stream, and the Briggses will be happy to cook up your catch the same day for dinner.

The guest rooms have peeled log walls and braided rugs. One has a fireplace and a window wall that seems to bring scenery inside. Most guests (never more than ten at a time) come to put city life behind them and rest; but the ranch offers a number of activities including a variety of trail rides through the neighboring mountains. Guests frequently arrange for jet-boat trips down the Salmon River (known locally and alarmingly as the "River of No Return") as well as trips to the Gold Rush ghost town of Ulysses. There are jeep trips into the surrounding wilderness, and trips to fishing holes along the nearby river. The riding, jeep trips, guide, and meals are included in the American Plan rates quoted in the chart-index at the end of this

volume. Indian Creek is a relaxing place where you are made to feel at home in the mountains by people who live there.

Accommodations: 4 cabins with private bath. *Driving Instructions:* The ranch is 12 miles downstream from North Fork, Idaho. Get specific instructions when making reservations. The ranch will pick guests up at the airport or in Salmon.

GRANDVIEW LODGE AND RESORT

Priest Lake, Idaho. Mailing address: Star Route Box 48, Nordman, ID 83848. 208-443-2433. *Innkeepers:* Bob and Dorothy Benscoter. Open all year.

Grandview Lodge and Resort is on Priest Lake in the Kaniksu National Forest of northern Idaho. The resort began with a few cabins in 1936. In 1965 a log cabin–style modern lodge with wide sun decks was built right out over the water. The lodge has its own marina, dock, and long stretch of beach. Large picture windows in the lodge face the south end of the lake with panoramic views of 12 miles of blue lake, a pine-forested shore, islands, and the snow-capped peaks of the northern Idaho mountains. The upper level of the lodge has guest rooms opening onto the sundecks overlooking the lake; other guest rooms are in the north wing, and all are furnished in a modern décor. Guest accommodations are also found in the cabins and condominium-like units with kitchens, bedrooms, baths, wood-burning fireplaces, and decks and porches overlooking the lawns and lakefront area.

In the lower level of the lodge, guests will find a cocktail lounge with a big fireplace. A window-walled dining room is just off the lounge, and both rooms have fine views of the wilderness lake and mountains. The lounge and dining room are open to guests and the public for all meals. The Grandview is a real resort with most of the resort trappings: dancing in the lounge, a heated outdoor swimming pool, full marine facilities (canoe, boat, and motor rentals), and even an amphibian airplane for scenic tours of the area. In the summer guests can water ski, swim, hike, fish, and boat around the 26-mile-long lake and its many secluded islands. The entire area is sparsely populated and offers the serenity of wilderness unmarked by roads and other signs of civilization.

Accommodations: 8 lodge rooms with private bath; 20 cottages. *Pets:* Not permitted. *Driving Instructions:* From Priest River go north on Route 57 for 36 miles to Reeder Bay Road. Then go east for 3½ miles on Reeder Bay Road to the lodge.

Salmon, Idaho

THE GREYHOUSE INN

U.S. 93, Salmon, Idaho. Mailing address: Star Route, Salmon, ID 83467. 208-756-3968. *Innkeepers:* Robert and Vera Slicton. Open June to October.

The Greyhouse Inn is a bed-and-breakfast inn that offers overnight housing in the foothills of the mountains leading up to the Continental Divide in the distance. The house with its multiangular roof was built in 1894 by a gentleman from Germany who operated the Salmon brewery and an ice house. Although the house originally stood in the village center of Salmon, a former mining town, it was moved in

1972 to its present location 12 miles outside the town. The Slictons, who have fully restored the nine-room Western farmhouse to its original turn-of-the-century flavor, maintain a small but thriving antiques business from its parlor. They also sell Western collectibles and locally made arts and crafts objects. Their expertise in identifying and restoring antiques of the mining period is reflected in the furnishings of the two guest rooms. Both rooms are equipped, in addition to the antique furniture, with electric baseboard heating and pot-bellied stoves and have floral design carpeting. Guests are welcome to read and relax in the first-floor sitting room, which always has a wood fire burning in its stove on fall and winter evenings. In the morning, Mrs. Slicton serves a Continental breakfast featuring home-baked muffins and cinnamon rolls.

Accommodations: 2 rooms sharing a hall bath. *Pets:* Not permitted. *Driving Instructions:* From Salmon, at the junction of Routes 93 and 28, take 93 south 12 miles to the inn. From Sun Valley, travel north on Route 75 to Route 93. Take 93 north about 50 miles. The inn is opposite highway marker 293.

Salmon is a former mining town in the Lemhi Valley on the western slopes of the Bitterroot Mountains. The Continental Divide is about 10 miles to the east. This was the first part of Idaho entered by any white man when the Lewis and Clark expedition came over the Divide. Gold was discovered in the 1860s, and Salmon City boomed as a supply center for the mining activities in the Western mountains. The town is a base for scenic float trips on the Middle Fork and Salmon rivers as well as for big-game hunting, steelhead fishing, and horseback riding. In the summer months there are jeep trips to local historic sites. Winter activities include skiing at *Lost Trail Pass* and cross-country skiing. The *Lemhi County Historical Society*, with collections covering the history of the county from Indian times to the present, is open April through October, Monday through Saturday. The *Salmon National Forest* completely surrounds the town for many miles and runs to the north, where it connects with the Nez Percé National Forest. There are numerous camping, hiking, fishing, and picnicking opportunities throughout the area. For further information on the national forest, write to Supervisor, Salmon National Forest, Forest Service Building, Salmon, ID 83467, or phone 208-756-2215.

Montana

Big Sky, Montana

LONE MOUNTAIN RANCH

P.O. Box 145, Big Sky, MT 59716. 406-995-4644. *Innkeepers:* Bob and Viv Schaap. Open June 1 to October 31 and December 1 to April 15.

The Lone Mountain Ranch, surrounded by tall pines, is on the edge of the Spanish Peak Wilderness Area, just around the corner from Big Sky. A mountain stream runs through the ranch. Lone Mountain rises over 11,000 feet in the Madison Range, which extends down into the nearby Yellowstone National Park. The big mountain presides over the ranch, and in late afternoons guests can walk to the top of a hill and watch the sun set behind its snow-capped peaks. The ranch house and its fifteen cabins are built of chinked native logs with authentic Western furnishings. Many antiques of the old West and Indian artifacts enhance the exposed-log interiors of the lodge, dining hall, and cabins. The fifteen log cabins, spread out along the mountain stream, are equipped with electric heat and modern private baths. Each has its own fireplace and plenty of wood. The cabins recently underwent extensive restoration and are comfortable and rather modern.

Guests and the innkeepers eat together in the Ranch's dining hall. It is centrally located to the cabins and has a casual old-West atmosphere and family-style meals. The furnishings are fashioned from rustic logs and blend with the Western look of the log building. The Schaaps cook up a wide variety of hearty ranch meals, each consisting of one entrée and many accompanying dishes. Dinners tend to be the talk of the trail, with much speculation about the evening's menu. These meals are passed around on huge platters in keeping with Western traditions, and there is always plenty for second helpings. Home-baked breads and desserts are favorites here.

There are horseback trips into the primitive high country of the Spanish Peaks, Gallatin National Forest, and Yellowstone. The Schaaps are concerned about the impact of too many horses on the high-country environment, so very few pack animals are used, and the equipment is very light. In addition to horseback trips of varying lengths and speeds, there are riding lessons for the less experienced and wilderness discovery walks emphasizing the area's geology and wildlife. Photography of the extraordinary flora and fauna is one of the specialties at Lone Mountain Ranch. The walks are led by an experienced, trained naturalist. Other activities include barbecue-supper rides, kayaking and trout fishing on the rivers of southeastern Montana near the ranch, and mule-drawn hayrides.

In winter the ranch becomes a Nordic ski center. The Schaaps groom and maintain a network of 35 miles of trails that begin right at the cabins. They offer Nordic ski equipment (rentals and sales), certified instruction, overnight guided tours to a back-country cabin 8 miles southwest of the ranch, and all-day ski trips into Yellowstone. The ideal powder and terrain are the envy of Nordic skiers the world over. The ranch offers all the ski services to day skiers as well as guests, and the only meal served to the public as well as lodgers is the winter skiers' luncheon special, featuring homemade soups, freshly baked breads, and an "all-you-can-eat" salad bar. The ranch has a Horsefly Saloon, offering the favorite skiers' drink, Viv's Hot Buttered Rum.

The Lone Mountain Ranch has room for just forty-five guests, which helps the Schaaps retain their friendly, personal service, making this a good vacation spot any time of the year. It is a very popular resort, and reservations should be made well in advance. The lodge has daily rates, but most guests register for one week or longer stays.

Accommodations: 15 rooms in cabins, all with private bath. *Pets:* Not permitted. *Driving Instructions:* Drive south from Bozeman Mountain on Route 191 for 35 miles. Turn right on the main road to Big Sky Resort and turn right again after 4 miles.

IZAAK WALTON INN

P.O. Box 675, Essex, MT 59916. Telephone: Ask operator to call Essex #1 via Great Falls, Montana. *Innkeepers:* Sid and Millie Goodrich. Open all year.

The Izaak Walton is a railroad hotel built in 1939 by the Great Northern Railway, which developed much of the area around and in Glacier National Park. The three-story, half-timbered building was bought in 1974 by the Goodriches, who began restoring it immediately. The result is a twenty room hotel that harks back to the days when the only access to this area was behind steam locomotives that chugged over trestles and through tunnels in the mountains. The railway operations continue to be an attraction for many guests, who enjoy watching the helper engines push the trains on their way to Marias Pass. The Goodriches gladly steer their guests to the best vantage points for photographs of the helper operation as well as the scenic trestles, overpasses, snow sheds, and tunnels.

The Goodriches' goal since taking over the hotel has been to maintain it in a comfortable way reminiscent of the past railroading days rather than to overmodernize it. The pine-paneled guest rooms on the top two floors have changed little since the hotel first opened. The original furniture is still in place in the rooms, each of which has a double and a single bed, a dresser, and two chairs. The rooms also have sinks and a tiny night table. Many have Stu Cassidy wildlife pictures on the walls. Four deluxe rooms have private bathrooms with shower and toilet.

On the first floor are the lounge, lobby, and dining room. The lobby now contains the post office for the tiny town of Essex. When Sid took over the hotel he managed to locate some old brass post-office boxes, installed them in the lobby, and became the postmaster. The job isn't exactly taxing. There are currently only twenty-five boxes in use. The town has three telephones (telephoning in is an adventure for your operator), so it is clear that overcrowding is not yet a problem here. Sid is a fine woodworker, and his larch burl table with legs made from old harrow tines graces the lobby. Sid is a weatherman too. The government installed a computer- and satellite-directed electronic rain gauge in Essex, and it is his job to tend it and mail in the

recording tapes once a month. Millie Goodrich, an avid collector of clocks, keeps many fine examples of antique timepieces of all sizes on view at the hotel. Railroad prints adorn many of the walls, including those of the basement bar and game room. Other railroad memorabilia and pieces of early equipment hang there for buffs to enjoy.

A sauna and a laundromat are available at the inn, and three meals are served daily to guests and the public. A standard menu is offered in the dining room, as well as daily specials, some of which include meat loaf, oven-baked chicken, and goulash. Hot apple pie à la mode is a house specialty. Meals may be started with the soup of the day, which might be split pea, bean, macaroni and tomato, fish chowder, or vegetable beef. All soups are made fresh and from scratch at the hotel.

The inn is a natural base for many types of outdoor recreation. In summer there is hiking on nearby trails in the Great Bear Wilderness area (more than 1,000 miles of trails) and the Bob Marshall Wilderness. Fishermen can walk to the Middle Fork River or hike to Marion Lake. There are many streams and lakes within easy driving distance in the surrounding wilderness and Glacier National Park. In the winter the inn is a major ski-touring center. It has doorstep access to miles of maintained (but ungroomed) cross-country skiing trails with Nordic Ski Patrolmen on duty. Skis and equipment are available for rental or purchase at the fully equipped ski shop.

The Izaak Walton is a remote railroad inn set against the backdrop of some of the best mountain scenery in the Rockies. The accommodations are not as luxurious as at many inns on the East or West Coast, but the setting and the congeniality of the innkeepers easily make up for that.

Accommodations: 20 rooms, 4 with private bath. *Pets:* Not permitted. *Driving Instructions:* The hotel is ½ mile off Route 2 between East Glacier and West Glacier, at the southern end of Glacier National Park. The only sign is the one for Essex, and it is easy to miss.

Essex, a minuscule town just off Route 2 at the south end of Glacier National Park, was in its heyday a bustling railroad community (no auto road was available for many years). There were about 400 residents in the 1920s and 1930s, and eight trains would stop there every day, according to an article in the *Hungry Horse News* published in Columbia Falls. Much of the area's development came about through the early efforts of the Great Northern Railway. Today, the focus is on recreation in all four seasons, and much of that centers on the Izaak Walton Hotel.

Glacier National Park, Montana

GLACIER PARK LODGE

East Glacier Park, MT 59434. Winter mailing address: Glacier Park Co., 1735 East Fort Lowell, Suite 7, Tucson, AZ 85719. 406-226-9311; 602-795-0377 in winter. *Innkeeper:* Don Hummel. Open early June through mid-September.

Glacier Park Lodge is considered by the Glacier Park Company to be "the Company's premier hotel." With the mountains forming a backdrop, you can swim in a heated pool, ride horseback across the valley, fish in glacier-fed lakes, relax in manicured annual and perennial gardens, or play golf on a 3,350-yard, nine-hole course.

As at the Old Faithful Inn at Yellowstone Park and the Many Glacier Hotel in this park, it is the cavernous lobby that sets the tone for the entire building. As you leave the gardens and enter the hotel, you are immediately struck by the size of the Douglas firs used in the lobby. The Great Northern Railway, builder of the hotel in 1912–14, shipped them from the Pacific Northwest on flatcars. Sixty trees still covered with their original bark and standing forty feet in height with an average diameter of forty inches serve as pillars. The largest, those that provide the interior support of the room, are 52 feet long and nearly six feet in diameter.

The extraordinary design for the building resulted from collaboration between S. I. Bartlett and Thomas D. MacMahon, two Chicago architects. McMahon went on to design the Many Glacier Hotel after completing work on Glacier Park Lodge. The guest rooms at this lodge have painted plaster walls and hardwood floors with throw rugs. About half face the mountains, and the remainder face the gardens. Most have balconies, except for those on the third floor. The dining room offers similar meals to those at the Many Glacier Hotel, but the entrées at the two establishments are never the same during a given period, which allows guests to move from hotel to hotel without repetition among their food choices.

Accommodations: 155 rooms with private bath. *Pets:* Permitted if leashed. *Driving Instructions:* Take U.S. 2 or Route 49 to East Glacier. The hotel is near the park's eastern entrance near East Glacier.

GRANITE PARK AND SPERRY CHALETS

Glacier National Park, Montana. Mailing address: Belton Chalets, Inc., P.O. Box 188, West Glacier, MT 59936. 406-888-5511. *Innkeepers:* Kay Luding and Lanny R. Luding. Open July 1 to Labor Day.

The Sperry and Granite Park Chalets are far and away the most remote and unusual lodgings in this book. Unlike the other accommodations in the park, these are both reached only by hiking trails, a trek of about four hours. Because they share most features and a common history, we have combined their description into a single writeup.

The chalets were built about 1914 by Jim and Louis Hill of the Great Northern Railway, the prime developer of the park. The buildings, except for their roofs, are built entirely of native rock and have survived their rugged environment virtually unscathed. Each has a dozen to two-dozen guest rooms outfitted with iron beds and rustic turn-of-the-century furniture. There are no private bathrooms. Restroom facilities are to be found in relatively recent detached buildings a short walk from the chalet. Rooms at Sperry are lighted with kerosene lamps, and each has a sink with cold running water. Rooms at Granite Park are lighted by candlelight, and sinks with cold water are on each

balcony. The combination lounge-dining rooms at the chalets are lighted with mantled lanterns. Meals are served informally at tables that bear the carved dates from early visitors, back to the first year the chalets opened. In each chalet four regular evening meals are rotated on a one-per-day basis. These include ham dinner, turkey, beef, and a fish dish. Each dinner is served with soup, salad, main entrée, and dessert.

Sperry Chalet is on the west side of Gunsight Mountain overlooking Lake McDonald and Whitefish Range. It is on a broad Alpine ledge, surrounded by peaks and waterfalls, in an area that abounds with mountain goats. It is not an infrequent experience to see as many as three dozen goats frolicking just outside the chalet, taking dust baths in the gravel. The main trail to the chalet leaves from the Lake McDonald Lodge parking lot. A spirit of informality prevails there, with frequent square dancing in the lounge after dinner. Most visitors who hike to Sperry take the side trip to Sperry Glacier, a 3.5-mile hike to the headwall (7,970 feet) and then up the stone steps to the top and across to the glacier. Saddle trips are available to Sperry from the Lake McDonald horse barn. Those who have their own horses may bring them to Sperry, where they may be tied to the hitching rail while the owners are guests at the chalet. Horses must pack in their own feed, as no grazing is allowed.

Granite Park Chalet is at the north end of the Garden Wall in the center of bear and deer country. On a lava outcropping, the chalet overlooks a mountain panorama that includes the Garden Wall, Logan Pass, the McDonald Valley, and the east side of the Livingston Range including some of the peaks in Canada. Trails to the chalet depart from several locations, including Logan Pass and the Swiftcurrent Campground. Saddle-horse trips to Granite Park are available from Many Glacier, coming over Swiftcurrent Pass, a very scenic horseback trip.

Accommodations: Rustic, remote cabins. *Pets:* Not permitted. *Driving Instructions:* Detailed hiking instructions are availalbe when reservations are made for either chalet. Point of departure depends on hiking trail chosen.

LAKE McDONALD LODGE

Lake McDonald, Glacier National Park, MT. Winter mailing address: Glacier Park Co., 1735 East Fort Lowell, Suite 7, Tucson, AZ 85719. 406-888-5431; 602-795-0377 in winter. *Innkeeper:* Don Hummel. Open early June through mid-September.

Lake McDonald Lodge is a clapboard hotel at the edge of the forest on the west side of the Continental Divide on the shores of the park's largest glacial lake. The hotel, the oldest surviving building in the Glacier Park Company system, is ringed with balconies that have peeled-log railings outside the doors to each room. Constructed of local material, the Lodge played a major role in the development of the park's visitor services by providing an early base for hiking and saddle-horse trips into the wilderness deep within the park. The site was originally a homestead owned by George Snyder, who built the region's first hotel in 1895, fifteen years before Congress established the park. That hotel was eventually moved from its site and converted into a camping-supply store, which burned in 1938. Union leader John L. Lewis purchased the land from Snyder in 1906 and built the present structure in 1913 and 1914. He designed it to be a hunting lodge for himself and his guests. The front of the hotel faces the lake, and all provisions and guests were transported 8 miles down the lake by boat.

Although guests may now arrive via a scenic drive along Lake McDonald through forests of cedar, lodgepole pine, and other evergreens; the hotel itself looks much as it did sixty years ago. The main lobby is three stories high, supported by cedars with their bark still intact. Both the lobby and the dining room contain trophies recollecting the lodge's history as a hunting headquarters. A bull moose watches over the stone fireplace, where a fire burns day and night throughout the summer. The artist C. R. Russell is said to have carved some of the figures still visible in the stone. In the fireplace can be seen the original kettle support, as this was the kitchen and heat source for the Lewis lodge. Keeping the moose company are other trophies, which include mountain sheep, deer, elk, and bald eagles.

Fuchsia hangs outside the hotel, and on the balconies are flower boxes of snapdragons, nasturtiums, and petunias. Rockers on the balconies overlook the lake and the mountains, which rise 5,000 feet above the water's edge. In addition to the lodge, cabins of various sizes are available for rental on a daily basis. The guest rooms at the hotel are similar in design and décor to the ones at Glacier Park Lodge. The menu is similar to the Many Glacier Hotel's, described below.

Accommodations: 101 rooms with private bath. *Pets:* Permitted if leashed. *Driving Instructions:* Take Route 2 to West Glacier and then the Going-to-the-Sun Road along Lake McDonald to the lodge, near the northeastern end of the lake.

MANY GLACIER HOTEL

Glacier National Park, Montana. Winter mailing address: Glacier Park Co., 1735 East Fort Lowell, Suite 7, Tucson, AZ 85719. 406-732-4311; 602-795-0377 in winter. *Innkeeper:* Ian B. Tippet. Open early June through mid-September.

The Many Glacier Hotel, with 191 rooms, is the largest hostelry owned and operated by the Glacier Park Company. At the foot of Swiftcurrent Lake and the Swiftcurrent Valley, the hotel is a good base for exploring the park in general and for other nearby activities such as hiking, horseback riding, trout fishing, and canoeing. Launch rides and horseback treks depart from the hotel grounds.

More than four hundred men were employed in the construction of the hotel over a two-year period in 1914 and 1915. Like most of the early park buildings, the Many Glacier Hotel was a project of the Great Northern Railway, which fostered national interest in tourism in the Wyoming and Montana area. The lumber to build the hotel was all felled and milled in the Swiftcurrent Valley. Designed by the Chicago architect Thomas McMahon, the hotel was built at a cost of $500,000. Roads to the site had to be constructed, a sawmill had to be built, and a quarry had to be developed just to handle the materials for the structure.

The lobby is the hotel's focal point, with a dozen or so logs at its perimeter supporting the three-story-high cathedral ceiling. In the center of the lobby is a free-standing fireplace with seats around it on all four sides. One entire wall of the lobby is plate glass, offering a view of Swiftcurrent Lake. An outdoor balcony gives guests an additional spot from which to enjoy the view. Because of the Alpine appearance of the hotel and its location in the center of what Theodore Roosevelt called the American Alps, it carries out a Swiss theme in much of its décor. The Swiss white cross on a red background and Swiss crest are emblazoned on every guest-room door, and the bellhops wear authentic Swiss lederhosen. For many years, the hotel has hired a student staff whose members combine service skills with an interest in the fine arts, particularly music and drama. Often guests have the opportunity to hear their waiters and waitresses perform choral works during the evening. The culmination of the summer's artistic activity is a play given by the staff toward the end of the season.

Numerous guest rooms at the Many Glacier Hotel face the lake

and have doors to their own wooden balconies. Most guest rooms have hardwood floors, although some have been carpeted. The rooms' atmosphere is rustic and comfortable with beamed ceilings and either painted-plaster or paneled walls. The furniture is largely heavy oak, but almost all of the original furnishings have been replaced in the more than sixty years since the hotel opened.

The dining-room menu changes throughout the season and from year to year. Typical meals start with radish boats and a choice of juice or soup. Entrées might include such items as mountain trout amandine; roast prime ribs; fried chicken; braised pot roast; coq au vin; grilled lamb chop; duckling à l'orange; and a choice of steaks. There are usually a salad plate and an omelet dish as well.

Accommodations: 191 rooms with private bath. *Pets:* Permitted on a leash in the hotel but not on trails in the park. *Driving Instructions:* The most direct access to the hotel is via the paved road from Babb, on the eastern border of the park. Take Route 89 to Babb.

PRINCE OF WALES HOTEL

Waterton Lakes National Park, Alberta, Canada. Winter mailing address: Glacier Park Co., 1735 East Fort Lowell, Suite 7, Tucson, AZ 85719. 403-859-2231; 602-795-0377 in winter. *Innkeeper:* Don Hummel. Open early June through mid-September.

Unlike the historic hotels on the American side of the border, the Prince of Wales, instead of having grown sideways with annexes, is still the tall, six-storied building that was constructed in 1926 and 1927 by the Great Northern Railway. It is on a hilltop above the township of Waterton, overlooking Waterton Lake, an international body of water that stretches more than 7 miles southward. On three sides are mountains that still bear the scars of successions of glaciers.

Lumber for the building (primarily fir and pine) was felled in Montana and processed at a sawmill and drying kiln on-site in Canada. Many of the logs were hand-hewn, and the quality of the workmanship is apparent in both the lobby and the dining room. Because of the severity of the winter winds, the building was anchored to its site by means of large cables installed from its loft, through the structure, and into the ground itself.

The hotel has steep sloping roofs, balconies for most rooms, and fine views in all directions. The view from the lobby is past the township and lake into the U.S. Rockies. Each evening a trio plays chamber music in the lobby. The many lake and lakeside activities include hiking, cruises, and horseback riding. Wildlife often approach the hotel and the township, where goats, sheep, and deer are frequently seen in the streets and gardens and on the hillsides. The décor of the guest rooms is essentially similar to that on the Glacier Park Company properties, and the menu is largely the same, with occasional Canadian touches such as Yorkshire pudding served with the roast beef.

Accommodations: 82 rooms. *Pets:* Permitted if leashed. *Driving Instructions:* Take Route 5 to Waterton Lakes in Waterton Lakes National Park.

Wyoming

Atlantic City, Wyoming

"MINER'S DELIGHT" INN AND RESTAURANT

Atlantic City, Wyoming. Mailing address: Lander, WY 82520. 307-332-3513. *Innkeepers:* Georgina and Paul Newman. Open May through New Year's Eve.

The "Miner's Delight" is really out of the way. The chinked log structures of the old hotel are at 7,660 feet in the Wind River Mountains of the Shoshone National Forest. Today, Atlantic City, an old gold mining town, boasts a population somewhere between ten and fifty, with an unknown number of ghosts. The "Miner's Delight" Restaurant's fame is countrywide. It is a nationally known gourmet restaurant with reviews in major American food magazines and newspapers. Ensconced in the 1895 log cabins that housed the old Carpenter's Hotel are the innkeepers, Paul and Gina Newman. It may be a great surprise to many to find such a fine restaurant in a tiny mountain ghost town, and it is an even bigger surprise to meet the cosmopolitan Newmans, an attractive, sociable New York couple. In the early 1960s, Paul had taken a year off from his high-powered Madison Avenue ad firm to reduce his high blood pressure, when he announced to Gina that they weren't going back to New York: "I'm

not going to die on Madison Avenue." When Gina recovered from the shock, she agreed, on the condition that they buy the old Carpenter Hotel. So it was that the two Newmans left their prestigious jobs, Gina as a magazine editor and Paul as an adman. They both enrolled in a variety of cooking schools, including James Beard's and Dione Lucas's, and even a sauce course at the Sorbonne. Amid dire predictions of "impossible," the place opened. The predictions of failure were based on solid reasoning: There was (and still is) no menu, the rates were fairly high, the food was to be international cuisine in a land of "I'll eat anything as long as it's steak," and the nearest customer was 35 miles away. The place was a fantastic success. Reservations must be made several weeks in advance for the very popular five-course dinner.

Although "Miner's Delight" is primarily a restaurant, it does maintain three small guest rooms in the hotel and three small, primitive chinked-log cabins for dinner guests who wish to spend the night. A Continental breakfast is included in the hotel rates. The hotel rooms have twin beds.

Each room in the inn has its own individual flair. Decorations are paintings, Paul's area photographs, antiques, and examples of old advertising art. Handwoven Navaho rugs are scattered on polished wood floors. The dining room, heated by an old army stove from Fort Stambaugh, has a wall of floor-to-ceiling windows and gray wood walls brightened by canary yellow bentwood chairs and flower-bedecked tables. The Saloon is a spacious room with pots of geraniums in front of the picture windows. The focal point of the room is an enormous native rock fireplace with several white couches and chairs grouped around it. The big bar has white Victorian bentwood chairs and tables and fresh flowers everywhere.

In the old days in Atlantic City, a "miner's delight" was a flash of gold in the pan; today, it has to mean the international cuisine of the Newmans' kitchen. Diners are treated to a full five-course dinner served from 6 P.M. to midnight. For a prix fixe, diners receive, by candlelight, a steady stream of dishes, beginning with appetizers that might include shrimp La Fonda, a fondue, coquilles Saint-Jacques, or the specialty of the house, a pâté maison. Soup could be a Senegalese curried chicken, a fresh broccoli, or black bean; the main courses run from an Italian manicotti with homemade noodles to a French coq au vin, Hawaiian pork, shrimp Creole, or a boned chicken Florentine. Fresh vegetables, salads, breads, and desserts complete the meal. This is indeed a special place.

Accommodations: 3 rooms, 1 with private bath; 3 cabins without indoor plumbing. *Children and Pets:* Pets are not permitted; children are allowed only on Sunday, including for meals. *Driving Instructions:* From Landers take Route 28 for about 29 miles to a left turn onto a dirt road marked Atlantic City. It is 3 miles over this well-graveled road to "Miner's Delight" and Atlantic City.

Cody, Wyoming

IRMA HOTEL

1192 Sheridan Avenue, Cody, WY 82414. 307-587-4221. *Innkeeper:* Rex Vanderhoff. Open all year.

Many people have built hotels. Bill Cody built a hotel too. He also built the town where it stands. In 1894, Cody heard tales of the Big Horn Basin just over the mountain from Sheridan, Wyoming, where he owned a lavish hotel. In the next few years he and several influential investors formed the basis of a company set up to develop and promote the area. Promotion was Cody's long suit. He had an almost magical sense of good theater. His Wild West Show was the smash hit of North America and Europe. At a performance in England, he had driven a stagecoach with the Prince of Wales riding shotgun and four crowned heads of European countries inside. It was therefore an easy matter for Cody to enlist financial supprt for his "Shoshone Land Development" project. By 1897 the rudiments of a town had been established and named "Cody" in his honor. In 1902 Buffalo Bill began construction of the Irma Hotel, named in honor of his only surviving daughter.

Cody was not a man to withhold money from any deserving project, and the Irma was no exception. In the end the project cost $80,000, a princely sum in 1902. Portions of the exterior walls of the Irma were constructed from locally gathered river stones, but most of the building was built of cut sandstone quarried nearby. In the years that followed, the Irma grew as did the town, with large additions in 1929 and a smaller addition in 1978.

Guests at the Irma may choose from rooms that retain the old-fashioned splendor of the Cody era and more modern rooms in the 1929 and 1978 additions. The fifteen "original" suites offered in the older section are formed from what were originally thirty guest rooms. The suites now each contain private bathrooms. During the restoration process, wallpapers similar to the original Victorian papers were chosen for each suite, and many of the original dressers, rockers, tables, and bedsteads were retained. New springs and mattresses were installed in each bed. Drapes were added to the rooms in place of the original pull shades, and carpeting was installed to cover the hardwood floors. Many of the bathrooms have retained claw-foot tubs and ornate marble wall sinks. Probably the most popular of these rooms is the Buffalo Bill Suite, where guests may sleep on the showman's original bed and enjoy the furnishings of the two-room suite he designed especially for himself. Each of the other fourteen suites in the old section of the Irma is named for a famous Wyoming hero.

On the Irma's first floor is its famous grill room. The dining room contains what is generally considered the most elaborate back bar in the West. The large cherrywood bar runs the length of the room and bears unusually fine carving and other ornamentation. The back bar was a gift to Cody from Queen Victoria in appreciation for his command performance in 1900. It was made in France, shipped to New York by steamer, then by rail to Red Lodge, Montana, and finally by horse-drawn freight wagon to Cody. In the early days of the Irma, the present dining room was the bar and billiards room. It now contains many early photographs showing cowboys standing at the bar while others shoot pool in the background.

The Irma serves a traditional selection of Western food at all three meals. The dinner menu features roast prime ribs of beef as a house specialty as well as five or six cuts of steak and four daily "steam table" specials. Typical of the latter are steamed Polish sausage with German hot potato salad, boiled baby beef tongue, barbecued spare ribs, and braised sirloin tips with noodles made in the Irma kitchen.

Accommodations: 41 rooms with private bath. *Driving Instructions:* Cody is at the intersection of Routes 14, 16, 20, 14A, and 120 in northwestern Wyoming. The Irma is in the center of town.

"What a great idea!" That's what lovers of country inns and country life are saying when they hear about **COUNTRY INNS NEWSLETTER.** They already know how delightful and romantic staying at a country inn can be, how attentive and friendly the innkeepers are, what a joy it is to escape the hustle & bustle of the city, airports and hotels. They enjoy the simple pleasures of countryside and village.

Now you, too, can discover a new world of simple pleasures, generous hospitality, good food and friendly, personal attention in **COUNTRY INNS NEWSLETTER.** Every month you'll find out about many inns, new and old, that we know you'll enjoy. We'll tell you all about them and their hosts, what's to do in the villages & surrounding countryside—walking, skiing, horseback-riding, sailing, antique-hunting, or just plain relaxing—whatever you'd like.

Not only that, you'll find many **exclusive discounts** for the readers of **COUNTRY INNS NEWSLETTER.** You'll save money on your stay at the inns, nearby restaurants, and more. You can have a very pleasant break from the usual resort and hotel scene and save money, too. And we'll be in touch with you every month by **first class mail**, a letter from your friends at **COUNTRY INNS NEWSLETTER.**

So subscribe today and you can start saving money immediately ...COUNTRY INNS NEWSLETTER is usually $25.00 a year, but if you use the coupon below, you'll **save $7.00** right away. Fill in the appropriate information and put the coupon in an envelope with your check or money order. Or use your convenient charge card.

- -

MAIL TO: **COUNTRY INNS NEWSLETTER,** 270 Lafayette Street, Room 1310, New York, N.Y. 10012

"What a great idea!" I'd (we'd) like a year's subscription to **COUNTRY INNS NEWSLETTER.** I understand that I will receive 10 issues a year by **1st Class Mail**.

☐ Check enclosed – $18.00 in the United States; $21.60 in Canada
        (usually $25 and $30, respectively)

☐ Please charge to ☐ MasterCharge ☐ Visa ☐ American Express

Account No. ☐☐☐☐☐☐☐☐☐☐☐☐☐☐☐☐☐☐☐

Interbank No._____Expiration Date_____

Signature_____

Name _____

Address _____

City _____ State_____ Zip_____

Make checks payable to **COUNTRY INNS NEWSLETTER**

Special discount offer expires October 31, 1981.

Evanston, Wyoming

PINE GABLES LODGE

1049 Center Street, Evanston, WY 82930. 307-789-2069. *Innkeepers:* Arthur and Jessie Monroe. Open all year.

The designation "lodge" in the name "Pine Gables Lodge" is something of a misnomer. The Monroes have restored a Victorian home in the style of many of the country inns found in northern and central California. Pine Gables was built as a private mansion in 1883 by A. V. Quinn, the owner of the local sawmill and an important local businessman and banker. Quinn chose a remote spot on a hillside on the outskirts of town for his two-story wood-frame house. In those days, the town did not extend to his door. Today, Evanston has grown up all around the house so that it now has a "downtown" location. Thanks to Quinn's lumbering connections, he was able to use the finest redwood siding to cover his house, which is dominated by the six gables that give the inn its name. A glassed-in sun parlor, added later, stretches two-thirds of the way across the front of the house, and a bay window completes that façade.

Guests enter the inn through the sun parlor. An antique shop occupies the front parlor to the right. The downstairs portion of the mansion is dominated by a 10- by 50-foot hallway with two-room parlors on each side. Mrs. Monroe collects oak furniture and early mining and farm tools. The parlor rooms to the left are used as guest rooms and are partitioned by large sliding doors, typical of buildings of the era and found in many New York City brownstones we have explored. The front guest room has the bay window that faces the street, and the rear guest room has a fireplace, not now in use but decorative. The rooms are carpeted and have dark mahogany four-poster beds, bevel-edged mirrored dressers, and other pieces from the late nineteenth century. The windows have lace curtains, which further establish the look of the period. Both the hallway and the parlor rooms have large brass chandeliers that were originally used as gaslight fixtures and later changed to use electricity. The parlor rooms, like the others on this floor, have 12-foot ceilings.

Guests climb a wide staircase to the second floor, where there are six more rooms, two with private bath. Each has a gabled dormer, and the front room has a bay window with a sitting area built in. Because a country inn is a novelty in this area of lifeless motels, many guests come away feeling that they have discovered a secret they never plan to share. Although the inn serves no meals, the Monroes will steer guests to several local restaurants.

Accommodations: 8 rooms, 2 with private bath. *Pets:* Not permitted. *Driving Instructions:* Evanston is at the junction of I-80 and Routes 89 and 150.

Grand Teton National Park, Wyoming

JENNY LAKE LODGE

Jenny Lake Loop Road, Grand Teton National Park, Wyoming. Mailing address: P.O. Box 240, Moran, WY 83013. 307-733-4647. *Innkeeper:* Emilio Perez. Open early June through Labor Day.

Jenny Lake Lodge grew up gradually from a homestead started in 1922 by Tony Grace. Won over by the beauty of the area, he began that year to build the log structures that remain today as part of the Jenny Lake Lodge complex. He planned a dude-ranch operation and built a main lodge and five guest cabins. He named his new business "Danny Ranch" after the daughter of a close friend who was one of his first guests. The original cabins continue to provide overnight accommodations, and the first lodge is the lounge in the present-day main building. In 1931, Grace sold his holdings to the Snake River Land Company, which had been sponsored by John D. Rockefeller, Jr., as part of his plan to create the Grand Teton National Park. Three years later, the ranch management was taken over by the Grand Teton Lodge Company, and the property was expanded by the addition of more cabins. In the mid-1950s the lodge complex was enlarged once again with a new kitchen for the main building and private bathrooms for each cabin.

The main building and the thirty cabins are built of logs. The lounge is constructed of logs for the walls and ceilings and native stone for the fireplace. The floors are all of hardwood, with throw rugs. Within each guest room are two easy chairs, a writing desk, a chest of drawers, and beds with headboards adapted from the original bedsteads. The rustic but comfortable accommodations harmonize with the natural setting. Each cabin bears the name of a local flower. Jenny Lake Lodge has five two-room fireplace suites that may be rented by couples but are a better buy for groups of three or four. There is no television and no bar. Although the lodge is rustic, there is an undercurrent of elegance, especially in the dining room, where perhaps more than elsewhere at Jenny Lake the Rockefeller touch of Rockresort management can best be felt. Because Jenny Lake operates on the Modified American Plan, guests have full choice of the breakfast and dinner menus. With advance reservations, the public is welcome at all three meals.

Breakfast consists of choices among melons and other fruits, eggs done any style, bacon, sausage, blueberry pancakes, and French toast. Picnic lunches are always available, as well as a dining-room luncheon menu. Every evening there is a different dinner menu resplendent with items from appetizers to desserts. Typical starters include a ramekin de fromage made with a Swiss cheese produced locally, king crab and salsify cocktail, chopped chicken liver with Bartlett pear, and cantaloupe Evelyn. Two freshly made soups are offered daily, followed by the choice of four entrées. Recent offerings included fillet of sole meunière with almonds, broiled mushrooms, and smoked ham on toast; duckling à l'orange; filet mignon bearnaise; veal parmesan; roast chicken forestière; and poached Columbia River salmon. A choice of two salads follows the entrée, and then come dessert and a beverage. Every Sunday the lodge has a very popular buffet dinner for which reservations are a must.

Jenny Lake Lodge is a short walk from the lake, and horseback riding is available at the Jenny Lake Stables nearby. The setting and small size of this rustic resort combine to produce a tranquillity not found in the more populated parts of Grand Teton National Park. All income from the lodge and the Grand Teton Lodge Company in general is used not only for their own operation but also to further the conservation activities of Jackson Hole Preserve, Inc., a nonprofit educational organization.

Accommodations: 30 cabins with private bath. *Driving Instructions:* The Lodge is 20 miles north of Jackson on Teton Park Inner Road.

Medicine Bow, Wyoming

VIRGINIAN HOTEL

P.O. Box 176, Medicine Bow, WY 82329. 307-379-2377. *Innkeepers:* J. D. McColley and Dick Mallory. Open all year.

For years, one of our closest friends used to tell us story after story of her early childhood spent in Medicine Bow, playing in the streets of the sleepy town, peering in the window of the old Diplodocus Bar (named for one of many dinosaur skeletons discovered nearby), and sliding down two stories of banisters at the Virginian Hotel, one of the few buildings in town of such height. We were thrilled to discover that the old Virginian Hotel is gradually being returned to its early Western style.

August Grimm set out to construct his "modern" hotel in 1909, seven years after Owen Wister had published the novel for which Grimm's hotel was named. The building was constructed of concrete blocks that were poured into molds on the construction site, a common practice at the turn of the century. The entire structure was completed in the fall of 1911. The white oak trim and stairwell were brought to the town in rough form by railroad and finished at the site. The leaded ceilings were manufactured in Saint Louis and also delivered by rail. The bar in the saloon was handmade from a load of pine and poplar off the back of a truck. Outside, a board sidewalk and a hitching post survive from an earlier era.

Gus Grimm, a gambler, had built the hotel to attract a sporting crowd to the town. He constructed it directly across from the Union Pacific Depot. Insofar as rail was then the primary form of travel and the fledgling Lincoln Highway was mostly a muddy rut from coast to coast, what better way to capitalize on the railroad than to build a place for weary passengers to spend their night, play some cards, and enjoy a libation or two? Rarely was the hotel empty in those early days. The trap door to the gaming room in the basement was rumored to require frequent oiling of the hinges lest they expose the participants below. When the cattle and horse drives came to town, the drovers sought a rare respite—a bed—at the Virginian. Of course, the buyers and sellers were quite wealthy and were known to turn a card or two. They occupied the rooms upstairs according to their means. The cowhands crowded into the top floor, where heat and water were not furnished. The price was right at 50 cents a night for the Spartan accommodations. The wheeler-dealers paid the princely sum of $5.00 to hang their spurs on the embossed doorknobs below.

In the 1940s, in conformity with fashion, ceilings were lowered, walls paneled, doors added, and fixtures changed. The Virginian did not escape such modernization. However, in the past five years, efforts have been made to return the Virginian to its original décor. Old pictures and descriptions in the local newspapers and from older community citizens have guided the restoration. The tile ceilings are being removed, and the leaded ceilings refurbished. Hardboard floors and wainscoting are being replaced. Renovation continues; the Owen Wister Dining Room has been completed and furnished with antiques. The second and third floors are finished, with the installation of period wallpapers, brass or iron beds, and early furnishings. Twelve of the rooms on the second and third floors consist of antique furnishings, each different from the other. An imposing brass four-poster more than a hundred years old graces the Wister Suite. Highboard walnut is found in another, oak in a third, and carved walnut in yet another. Two rooms have cavalry bunks from the Medicine Bow supply depot of the 1870s, and all the rooms contain commodes, hardwood dressers, or old antique wardrobes. The feeling of the rooms captures the Westward movement. Throughout are the memories of gamblers, gunfighters, cattle barons, and homesteaders. In addition to the hotel rooms, there are nineteen in an adjacent motel.

Food is served at the Virginian in the coffee shop (open 6 A.M. to 10 P.M.) and in the dining room. The coffee shop offers a wide selection of sandwiches and grill items as well as several complete dinners. The dining room, named in honor of Owen Wister, has eight offerings, including ribs, steaks, chops, and seafood.

Accommodations: 20 hotel rooms, sharing baths; 19 motel rooms with private bath. *Pets:* Not permitted in the hotel rooms. *Driving Instructions:* Take U.S. 30-287 north from Laramie or Walcott to Medicine Bow, or take Route 287 south from Casper to Route 487, which leads directly to Medicine Bow.

The area around Medicine Bow has borne Indian names of similar meaning for centuries in consequence of the excellent bow and arrow materials gathered from the banks of the Medicine Bow River. The village sprang up around a supply point for the Union Pacific Railroad, and by 1876 the town had its first elementary school. In the latter half of the nineteenth century and the first part of this century, livestock kept the town alive. The arrival of the author Owen Wister in the 1880s, however, was to immortalize the town. He spent twenty-five years collecting stories of the Old West and in the process published several novels. According to legend, an early county deputy sheriff was insulted during a poker game and retorted, "When you call me that, smile." The remark found its way into Wister's most famous novel, *The Virginian*. The book, set in the Medicine Bow area, eventually brought much fame to the town through its adaptation into a television series in the 1960s.

When the livestock trade dwindled, the town's businesses shrank. They enjoyed periodic revivals with the discovery of coal, oil, and uranium, as well as the largest collection of dinosaur bones ever found in the country.

HEART SIX GUEST RANCH

Jackson Hole–Moran, Wyoming. Mailing address: P.O. Box 70, Moran, WY 83013. 307-543-2477 or 307-733-6650. *Innkeeper:* Carol Beeston. Open all year.

Heart Six Guest Ranch comprises a number of rustic peeled-log buildings set in the Buffalo River Valley with the Grand Tetons rising high in the background. The warmth of natural wood predominates. The lounge in the main lodge is typical of Heart Six. The lines are simple with an exposed-beam wooden ceiling, large picture windows overlooking the valley, and a large stone fireplace centered on the long exterior wall. That wall, like most exterior walls of the lodge and cabins, consists of chinked peeled logs exposed on the outside and covered with pine paneling on the interior. The floors of finished natural wood bear the patina of age.

The main lodge has two dining rooms and a modern kitchen, where family-style ranch meals are prepared. Dinners range from steak cookouts held on the Thursday evening trail rides and a roast beef dinner to the traditional Sunday turkey dinner with all the fixings. Breakfasts include the only choices offered for dining at Heart Six: eggs any style, French toast, or pancakes and bacon. Once a week there is a breakfast cookout where sourdough hotcakes, bacon, eggs, and coffee are cooked over an open fire.

Cabin rooms at Heart Six maintain the rustic flavor of the lodge but have wall-to-wall carpeting instead of exposed wood floors. The typical room has a double bed with several chairs and a night table. Some of the larger units have one or two bedrooms, a living room, private bathroom with tub and shower, and a picture window facing the Grand Tetons. There are also rooms in the lodge itself, with private baths. The relatively small size keeps the atmosphere appropriately friendly and "innlike." Rooms do not have telephones or television.

Activities on the ranch include horseback riding on timbered mountain trails and trout fishing in either the local lakes or mountain streams. Guests at the ranch have an opportunity to take a scenic float trip down the Snake River on a large pontoon boat. The Snake offers what we consider to be the finest float trips in the Rockies. Wildlife abound, and most visitors go home with pictures of nesting eagles and moose browsing on underwater vegetation. Picnic lunches are served at the halfway point on these trips. Guests in residence on Saturday nights are provided with transportation to the weekly evening rodeo in Jackson. The ranch has a resident children's activities director who is a professional in the field. All the activities and meals are included in the basic weekly rate, but there are some optional additional activities, such as overnight pack trips into the wilderness, that result in additional charges. The ranch is close enough to both Grand Teton National Park (4 miles) and Yellowstone (30 miles) to permit tours of either park in one-day trips. Guests should remember that the nearest full-service shopping is at Jackson, and they should stock up with things like wine or liquor there before coming.

Accommodations: 15 rooms (in cabins and lodge), with private bath. *Pets:* Not permitted. *Driving Instructions:* Routes 26, 89, and 187 north of Jackson 30 miles to Moran Junction, then east 5 miles to Buffalo Valley Road. Turn on Buffalo Valley and drive 1½ miles to Heart Six.

Saratoga, Wyoming

MEDICINE BOW LODGE GUEST RANCH

Route 130, Saratoga, Wyoming. Mailing address: P.O. Box 752, Saratoga, WY 82331. 307-326-5439. *Innkeepers:* John and Teri Owens. Open from Memorial Day weekend to mid-September and from mid-December to Easter weekend.

Medicine Bow Lodge stands on 75 acres in the Medicine Bow National Forest at an altitude of 8,000 feet. The lodge is in a remote area, 20 miles southeast of Saratoga. The Sierra Madre and Medicine Bow mountain ranges provide a panoramic backdrop for the high-plains Platte Valley. Roaming herds of deer, elk, and antelope are familiar sights at the lodge, as are bear, beaver, fox, and coyote in the surrounding hills. Two mountain trout streams cross the property and offer excellent fishing. The main lodge and eight cabins are mountain-style log structures built in the early 1920s. The chinked-log cabins, each with a private modern bath and propane heat, sleep up to nine people. The big lodge is a rustic building containing a sunny dining room, a kitchen, and a spacious living room with a fire in its stone fireplace. It is decorated throughout with animal skins and mounted trophies.

Three ranch-style Western meals are served in the dining room. The menu is completely up to the chef's discretion; he has spent many years satisfying appetites sharpened by plenty of fresh mountain air and outdoor activities, so expect big plates filled with good, hearty food. Accompanying the meals are homemade breads, rolls, and pastries. The public can dine here for lunch or dinner with advance reservations. Guests are entertained by the brightly colored hummingbirds that come and go at the dining room window's feeders. Horses graze freely by the mountain stream that flows just a few feet from the lodge. Horseback riding is the featured attraction here, and the horses are surefooted creatures well used to the mountain and forest trails.

In winter the cross-country skiing and snowmobiling at the ranch are excellent. Winters there are quite exciting, as the temperature occasionally drops well below zero. The cabins at such times have no plumbing, and guests must use the bath facilities in the lodge nearby. It is a time for enjoying a songfest around the fire and swapping tales of adventures experienced along the trails of Medicine Bow National Forest.

Accommodations: 8 cabins with private bath. *Driving Instructions:* From Saratoga take Routes 130 and 230 south for 8 miles. Turn east on Route 130 when it leaves Route 230. Go 12 miles to the lodge entrance on the south side of the highway. There are signs to the lodge at the entrance.

Saratoga is a town of slightly more than 1,000 in the southeastern part of the state, about 25 miles from the Colorado border. Saratoga's fame was initially derived from its plentiful hot medicinal springs. There is excellent trout fishing in the North Platte River, which passes through the town. Float trips may be arranged down the same river. For more information about Saratoga, contact the Chamber of Commerce at 207 East Walnut, Saratoga, WY 82331.

Shoshone National Forest, Wyoming

ABSAROKA MOUNTAIN LODGE

Off Routes 14, 16, 20, Shoshone National Forest, Wyoming. Mailing address: P.O. Box 7, Cody, WY 82414. 307-587-3963. *Innkeepers:* Michael and Caroline Rueffert. Open all year.

The Absaroka Mountain Lodge is in a small mountain valley in the heart of the Shoshone National Forest, surrounded by the wilderness of the Absaroka Mountains. This rustic lodge has the look of a remote wilderness hunting camp but is only 300 yards off the road and just ten minutes from the east entrance of Yellowstone National Park. The road, running along the Wapiti Valley and the North Fork of the Shoshone River, is considered by many to be "the most scenic 50 miles in the world." It runs from historic Cody, through the Shoshone Canyon, to Yellowstone.

Here in the valley the original homestead cabin, constructed out of chinked logs, was built in 1904. It is a well-built structure still containing the original fireplace, which the innkeepers say has fires only on special occasions. The homestead now houses the dining room. In the 1930s the lodge, in the same chinked-log construction, was attached. Both parts are rustic and inviting; the lodge is a good place to relax in front of the hearth, sip hot apple cider, and relive the day's adventures of wilderness hiking and fishing. The log construction is exposed in the interior. The hardwood floors are covered with hand-woven Indian rugs, and the collection of handmade Western furniture enhances the mountain atmosphere. The dining room has heavy wooden tables and comfortable handmade chairs of chunky wood with laced rawhide seats and backs, much like the snowshoe furniture of the Northeast. Lodge furnishings consist of some rawhide pieces and tables, chairs, and couches of bark-stripped logs and smaller branches with soft cushions. Both the dining room and lodge walls are decked with hunting trophies.

The lodge has several winterized log cabins for guests. The mountain rooms are set in woods of Douglas fir and aspens along Gunbarrel Creek. Two cabins have original furnishings with comfortable handmade beds and chairs of the same log style as those in the lodge. The remaining cabins have two bedrooms, each of which has a private entrance and bath. These rooms are rather small, with carpeting and newer furniture in a Western style.

Breakfasts and dinners are served in the 1904 dining room. The restaurant is open to guests and the public. Wyoming breakfasts start the day with selections of eggs, sausages, ham, and bacon, along with sourdough buckwheat pancakes, special French toast, lots of maple syrup, and hot coffee and tea. Dinners consist of traditional American foods in big portions. There are a salad bar and a daily choice of a variety of meats such as steaks barbecued outdoors, rainbow trout (the house specialty), fried chicken, beef stew, and others. A selection of liquors, wines, and beers is available.

For peace and quiet, there is some of the most scenic hiking or cross-country skiing country in the West. The downhill ski area is just 8 miles away, and the lodge rents cross-country ski equipment to guests at a 28 percent discount. The Ruefferts will gladly arrange for pack trips, fishing trips, and boating excursions.

Accommodations: 13 cabin rooms with private bath. *Driving Instructions:* The lodge is in the heart of the Shoshone National Forest near the east gate of Yellowstone National Park. Go 40 miles west of Cody on Routes 14, 16, 20.

BILL CODY'S RANCH INN

Routes 14, 16, 20, Shoshone National Forest, Wyoming. Mailing address: P.O. Box 1390, Cody, WY 82414. 307-587-2097. *Innkeepers:* Bill and Barbara Cody. Open May 1 to September 30 and December 15 to March 15.

Bill Cody's Ranch is about midway between Cody and Yellowstone National Park in the heart of the northern section of Shoshone National Forest. Operated by the grandson of the famous folk hero and Western showman, the ranch is near the mouth of a canyon that runs back about 5 miles to Ptarmigan Mountain rising more than 12,000 feet. As you arrive at the ranch you are greeted by a sight that is rare in the Wyoming mountains. In front of the main lodge is a groomed lawn bordered by a flower garden that is a riot of color from spring to fall. The garden fence is a chain woven of deer and elk antlers.

The Ranch comprises about a dozen buildings arranged in a horseshoe shape. At the mouth of the horseshoe is the main lodge, with lounge, living room, dining room, the ranch kitchen, and one sleeping unit. This building, like all buildings on the ranch, is made of peeled logs, the only building material permitted by the National Forest Service at Shoshone. The lounge on the newly enclosed front porch has a beer bar only. Guests who wish to drink anything stronger must bring it with them. A native stone fireplace encrusted with local geodes in the living room of the lodge contrasts nicely with the peeled lodge-pole pine logs. The lodge is more than 70 feet long, and a single tree provided the ridge pole that spans the roof. The Western atmosphere of the lodge is enhanced by the electrified kerosene lanterns, Navaho rugs, an antique piano, and the numerous mounted heads of deer, elk, and mountain sheep. Most rooms in the lodge and the guest cabins have unusual hand-crafted lamps made of native knobbled pine. (Knobbling is a form of burl-like response to a cancerous disease that strikes the local pines.) The dining room has been paneled with tongue-and-groove knotty pine and is decorated with examples of Western art and Western memorabilia, such as a collection of peace pipes. The art displayed throughout the ranch rooms, including all the guest cabins, represents many Western artists, several of whom, like Harold Hopkinson, James Baman, George Dee Smith, and Arthur Putnam, have achieved national prominence. The décor combines with Barbara and Bill's hospitality to make guests feel at home.

The dining room, open to both guests and the public, has an à la carte menu and offers three meals daily. For dinner there are two daily specials such as baked ham, spaghetti, macaroni and cheese with ham, or stew, as well as mountain trout and three regular steaks. On Sunday there is a steak or chili cookout.

Guests are accommodated in several cabins, most of which are divided into two separate sleeping quarters. Typical accommodations include a double or queen-size bed with a custom-made headboard, a couch that converts to a twin bed, an easy chair, a writing desk and chair, and a side table with a knobbled-pine lamp. A three-story chalet-style building set into the hillside contains a two-floor family apartment with a separate suite below that may be rented together with the top two floors or as a separate unit. Some of the cabins face the creek that meanders through the property, and others back onto it. The one guest room in the main lodge is actually a small suite with a sleeping porch off the main room.

Summer ranch activities include horseback riding over well-maintained trails with experienced ranch guides. There is a great variety of wilderness riding here from wooded creek bottom to mountaintop. There is no limit on riding, and there are daily picnic rides and cookouts. Many guests enjoy other activities such as hiking on local trails, taking float trips down the Shoshone River, or enjoying the unlimited wonders of Yellowstone or the several museums and shopping places in and around Cody. In the winter the ranch takes its guests to the Sleeping Giant Ski Area, which is just a few minutes away. There are also virtually unlimited cross-country skiing and several new wilderness snowmobile trails through Yellowstone.

Accommodations: 16 rooms, mostly in cabins, with private bath. *Pets:* Sometimes permitted with advance notice. *Driving Instructions:* The ranch is a half-mile off Routes 14, 16, and 20 and about 25 miles from both Cody and Yellowstone National Park.

GOFF CREEK LODGE

Routes 14, 16, and 20, Shoshone National Forest, Wyoming. Mailing address: P.O. Box 155, Cody, WY 82414. 307-587-3753. *Innkeepers:* Paul and Gloria Schmitt. Open mid-May through mid-October.

Goff Creek Lodge is in the beautiful Wapiti Valley, just 10 miles from the east entrance of Yellowstone National Park. Goff Creek was first occupied in 1905 by John Goff, who used it as his hunting camp. The renowned hunting guide and buffalo hunter acted as the personal guide to President Theodore Roosevelt on his American big-game hunts and was highly spoken of in Roosevelt's memoirs as both a personal friend and an outstanding guide.

Goff Creek Lodge consists of a main lodge and a group of log cabins in the pine and fir timber of the Absaroka Rockies, between two mountain ridges bounding Goff Creek. The creek, a white-water, spring-fed mountain stream, flows past the cabins on its way to the Shoshone River below. The lodge was built in 1910 and was completely renovated about fifteen years ago. The main lodge has a warm, Western feeling created by its peeled-log walls, exposed-log and plank ceilings and ranch-style oak furniture. Guests gather here for dinner, which is served at tables under the wagon-wheel-and-hurricane-lamp chandelier. On cool days a fire burns in the stone fireplace in the center of one wall. The dinner menu offers turkey, chicken, ham steak, fried shrimp, and boneless mountain trout, a lodge specialty. Accompanying the meal are homemade breads and, for dessert, a selection of fresh cakes. Lucky fishermen may have their catch of the local cutthroat trout prepared for either breakfast or dinner. Because the lodge is such a convenient base for exploring Yellowstone National Park, the cook will gladly pack a box lunch to be enjoyed at a park picnic area later in the day. The lounge continues the Western motif with lamps made from boots, authentic Navaho rugs, and hunting trophies and Indian artifacts on display.

The cabins, most containing two guest rooms, are of the peeled-log construction mandated in the national forest. Each has either wall-to-wall or area carpeting, pine-paneled walls decorated with horse and other Western pictures, and, like the lodge, exposed-beam and plank ceilings. Furnishings are simple, in keeping with the rooms' character.

Accommodations: 14 rooms with private bath. *Driving Instructions:* The lodge is 41 miles west of Cody on Routes 14, 16, and 20.

ELEPHANT HEAD LODGE

P.O. Box C, Wapiti, WY 82450. 307-587-3980. *Innkeepers:* Robert R. and Debra C. Houle. Open May 1 to October 1.

The Elephant Head Lodge, named for its proximity to a local rock formation, is a half-moon arrangement of ten cottages around a very early log cabin lodge and dining room. The lodge and the "honeymoon" cabin were both built in 1910 by Buffalo Bill's niece and her husband. The lodge has been maintained with its original peeled-log interior and exterior, with a large stone fireplace at one end and a bar at the other. Flanked by rock cliffs on two sides and surrounded by pine trees, the lodge is but a few feet from the trout-filled Shoshone River.

Each of the ten cabins exhibits the log exterior mandated by the national forest. Many of the cabins have wall-to-wall carpeting, and most have peeled-log furniture, an unusual type of furniture handmade from 5-inch-diameter pine logs assembled into beds and tables without the use of nails. Needless to say, the beds are massive. The cabins all have individually controlled heat and private bathrooms, and the honeymoon cabin has its own working fireplace. There is also a fireplace in the main lodge, with a fire going in the early morning and the evening every day.

The log dining room, next to the main lodge, serves three meals daily, of which both breakfast and dinner are served to the public as well as guests. The menu consists of chopped sirloin with creamy mushroom sauce, Rocky Mountain rainbow trout with lemon slices, deep-fried shrimp, and a special of the day such as a stew, meat loaf, or lasagna. Breads and desserts are made on the premises.

Activities at the Elephant Head Lodge include wilderness trail rides on horseback, fishing in the Shoshone River, and backpacking or exploring in Yellowstone Park, 11 miles from the lodge. Indian artifacts are still found in the area, and an Indian mummy was found 3 miles from the lodge in 1973. Local game includes moose, elk, deer, and bear.

Accommodations: 10 cabins with private bath. *Driving Instructions:* The lodge is on Routes 14, 16, and 20 about 40 miles west of Cody and 11 miles east of the east entrance of Yellowstone Park.

OLD FAITHFUL INN

Yellowstone National Park, WY 82190. 307-344-7321. *Innkeeper:* The Yellowstone Park Division of TWA Services. Open early May to mid-October.

The Old Faithful Inn is actually the second one built near the famous geyser. The original burned in 1894 and was not immediately replaced because a regulation prohibited building within ¼ mile of any park attraction. The original had been illegally placed closer, and backers of the hotel felt that to build farther away would detract from the hotel's popularity. Finally the ruling was changed and plans were laid to construct the present hotel ⅛ mile from Old Faithful.

In 1902 a young architect, Robert C. Reamer, was selected to design the new hotel. Construction began in 1903 and continued through the long bitter winter until completion in 1904, just before the park opened that year. The primary building materials were native to the area. All the logs and the twisted supports so clearly seen in the lobby and throughout the old portions were gathered nearby. The stone, including the 500 tons required for the huge fireplace, was quarried on the road to West Thumb. The original building contained 140 rooms and was described as the largest log hotel in existence.

Entrance doors to the inn are made of massive split logs and have hand-wrought hardware. The central lobby, the showplace of the hotel, is 64 feet square and rises 85 feet to the ridge pole. Dormer windows, later to become one of Reamer's trademarks, light the ceiling. Four overhanging balconies descend the walls and offer views of the large rough-stone fireplace and its big clock embedded in the stone. The clock keeps accurate time even today, after seventy years. The clock, the copper light fixtures, and all other hardware in the building were designed by Reamer and wrought by a blacksmith on the site.

Over the years, the pressures of overflow crowds visiting the park required two wings to be constructed on the original building. Both the 1913 and the 1928 wings were designed by Reamer to harmonize with his original plan. The inn can accommodate a total of 90,000 visitors each season.

There are three types of rooms at Old Faithful Inn. The newest are

the deluxe rooms with private bath. They are in the latest wing and have been thoroughly modernized. The "private bath" rooms are a compromise between fully modernized and rustic. They sometimes have the peeled-log walls exposed but have fully modern baths. However, the rooms in the original hotel are the most historic and reminiscent of a visit to Yellowstone at the turn of the century. These have split-log doors, exposed peeled-log interiors, and, in many cases, the original iron or brass beds. The rooms, lighted by early wall sconces, have all been carpeted. Many overlook the geyser, and some have bay windows with sitting areas. These rooms are in great demand, but if guests request them well in advance, the staff at the hotel will try to accommodate the request. In any event, there is a second-floor outdoor balcony that has a fine view of the geyser and a full set of wicker furniture for relaxed geyser-watching.

The dining rooms in each of the Yellowstone Park hotels and lodges have a menu that is redesigned for each season. For this reason it is impossible to predict exactly what food services will be available in any specific place. In general, however, each has a full menu.

Accommodations: 364 rooms, 196 with private bath. *Driving Instructions:* The inn is only yards from the Old Faithful geyser, just off the southwestern Grand Loop road that circles the interior of the park. Access to the road is through any of the five main gates.

Index

WITH ROOM-RATE AND CREDIT-CARD INFORMATION

Inns are listed in the chart that follows. In general, rates given are for two persons unless otherwise stated. Single travelers should inquire about special rates. The following abbreviations are used throughout the chart:

dbl. = double. These rates are for two persons in a room.

dbl. oc. = double occupancy. These rates depend on two persons being registered for the room. Rentals of the room by a single guest will usually involve a different rate basis.

EP = European Plan, either no meals or a simple Continental breakfast.

MAP = Modified American Plan: rates include dinner and breakfast. Readers should confirm if stated rates are per person or per couple.

AP = American Plan: rates include all meals. Readers should confirm if stated rates are per person or per couple.

Credit-Card Abbreviations

AE = American Express

CB = Carte Blanche

DC = Diners Club

MC = Master Charge

V = Visa

Important: All rates are the most recent available but are subject to change. Check with the inn before making reservations.

Absaroka Mountain Lodge, 169; Rates: $27 dbl. EP; MC, V

Anderson House, The, 48; Rates: $23 to $35 dbl. EP; DC, MC, V

Baker's Manor Guest House, 123; Rates: $13 dbl. EP

Balloon Ranch, The, 114; Rates: $170 dbl. AP

Bay Shore Inn, 75; Rates: $28 to $53 dbl. EP; MAP available

Beaumont Hotel, 85; Rates: $13 to $16 dbl. EP

Bel-Horst Inn, 93; Rates: $18 dbl. EP

Bill Cody's Ranch Inn, 171; Rates: $60 to $68 dbl. oc. AP; AE, CB, DC, Exxon, MC, Sohio, V

Blue Bell Lodge and Resort, 103; Rates: $28 to $35 dbl. EP; MC, V

Botsford Inn, 26; Rates: $30 to $45 dbl. EP; AE, MC, V

Buxton Inn, The, 51; Rates: $25 to $30 dbl. EP; MC, V

Cascade Lodge, 38; Rates: $32 dbl. EP

Chateau Madeleine, 69; Rates: $65 to $80 dbl. AP

Colonial Guest House, 4; Rates: $26 dbl. EP

Colonial Inn, 10; Rates: $24 dbl. EP

Dearborn Inn, The, 24; Rates: $58 to $72 dbl. EP; AE, DC, MC, V

Die Heimat Motor Hotel, 77; Rates: $25 to $30 dbl. EP

Elephant Head Lodge, 174; Rates: $30 to $50 dbl. EP; MC, V

Fort Robinson State Park Lodge and Cabins, 95; Rates: $12 to $14 dbl. EP; MC, V

General Palmer House, 116; Rates: $44 dbl. EP; AE, DC, Exxon, MC, V

Glacier Park Lodge, 144; Rates: $35 to $40 dbl. EP

Goff Creek Lodge, 173; Rates: $30 to $49 dbl. EP; AP available; AE, MC, V

Golden Lamb, The, 55; Rates: $36 dbl. EP; AE, MC, V

Grand Hotel, 30; Rates: $65 to $105 per person, dbl. oc. AP

Grand Imperial Hotel, 128; Rates: $24 to $38 dbl. EP; AE, MC, V

Grandview Lodge and Resort, 136; Rates: $28 to $69 dbl. EP; MC, V

Granite Park and Sperry Chalets, 145; call for current rates

Granville Inn, The, 53; Rates: $38 dbl. EP; MC, V

Greunke's Inn, 57; Rates: $20 to $32 dbl. EP;

Greyhouse Inn, The, 137; Rates: $25 dbl. EP

Griffin Inn, The, 62; call for current rates

Gunflint Lodge, 40; Rates: $48 per person, dbl. oc. EP; MC, V

Harbour Inn, 28; Rates: $60 to $64 dbl. MAP

Hardesty House, 83; Rates: $12 to $15 dbl. EP

Harlan House, 81; call for current rates

Heart Six Guest Ranch, 166; Rates: $65 to $90 per person AP; AE, MC, V

Hearthstone Inn, The, 108; Rates: $38 to $58 dbl. EP; MC, V

Heidel House Resort and Conference Center, 65; Rates: $50 to $59 dbl. EP; AE, MC, V

Historic Redstone Inn, The, 126; Rates: $33 to $37 dbl. EP; MC, V

Hobson's Bluffdale, 3; Rates: $31.50 per person AP; children less

Hotel Boulderado, 106; call for current rates

Hotel du Nord, 73; Rates: $30 to $60 dbl. EP

Hotel Nauvoo, 12; call for current rates

Hotel Powers, 97; Rates: $14 dbl. EP; AE, CB, DC, MC, V

Hotel St. Elmo, 124; Rates: $30 to $50 dbl. EP; MC, V

Imperial Hotel, 112; Rates: $27 dbl. EP; AE, DC, MC, V

Indian Creek Guest Ranch, 134; Rates: $80 per person EP; V

Inn St. Gemme Beauvais, The, 91; call for current rates

Irma Hotel, 157; Rates: $26 per person dbl. oc. AP; AE, MC, V

Iroquois, The, 32; Rates: $45 to $120 dbl. EP; MC, V

Izaak Walton Inn, 141; Rates: $20 dbl. EP; MC, V

Jamieson House, 71; Rates: $45 to $55 dbl. EP

Jenny Lake Lodge, 161; Rates: $150 dbl. MAP

La-Pat Hotel, 132; Rates: $11 to $15 dbl. EP; AE, MC, V

Lake McDonald Lodge, 148; Rates: $27 to $39 dbl. EP
Lone Mountain Ranch, 139; Rates: $56 dbl. EP; MC, V
Lowell Inn, 46; Rates: $59 to $99 dbl. EP; MC, V
Manning Hotel, 79; call for current rates
Mansion, The, 59; Rates: $125 dbl. AP
Many Glacier Hotel, 150; Rates: $35 to $39 dbl. EP
Medicine Bow Lodge Guest Ranch, 167; call for current rates; MC, V
"Miner's Delight" Inn and Restaurant, 154; Rates: $38 dbl. EP
National House Inn, The, 34; Rates: $45 dbl. EP
New Harmony Inn, The, 20; call for current rates; AE, CB, DC, MC, V
New Sheridan Hotel and Bar, 130; Rates: $85 to $56 dbl. AP; AE, MC, V
Old Faithful Inn, 175; Rates: $28 to $45 dbl. EP; AE, DC, MC, V
Old Rittenhouse Inn, 60; Rates: $35 to $45 dbl. EP
Outlook Lodge, 121; call for current rates; MC
Palmer Gulch Lodge, 105; Rates: $25 dbl. EP; MC, V
Palmer House Hotel and Restaurant, 44; Rates: $15 per person dbl. EP
Peck House, 119; Rates: $25 to $30 dbl. EP; AE, MC, V
Pine Gables Lodge, 159; Rates: $29 to $33 dbl. EP
Potawatomi Inn, 14; Rates: $25 to $28 dbl. EP
Prince of Wales Hotel, 152; Rates: $40 to $46 dbl. EP
Rosalea's Hotel, 86; Rates: $15 to $30 per person EP
Rough Riders Hotel, 99; Rates: $36 dbl. EP; AE, MC, V
St. Clair Inn, 36; Rates: $45 dbl. EP; AE, MC, V
Schumacher's New Prague Hotel, 42; Rates: $55 to $65 dbl. EP, Sun-Thurs;
     $75 to $85 weekends.
Seven Pines Lodge and Trout Preserve, 67; Rates: $47.50 per person AP
Sherman House Restaurant and Inn, 16; Rates: $14 to $50 dbl. EP
Skoglund Farm, 101; Rates: $15 per person MAP
Soward Ranch, 111; Rates: from $20 dbl. EP
Spring Mill Inn, 19; Rates: $25 dbl. EP; MC, V
Stillman Manor, 6; Rates: $35 dbl. EP; MC, V
Strater Hotel, 117; Rates: $34 to $55 dbl. EP; AE, CB, DC, MC, V
Terrace Inn, The, 22; Rates: $15 to $30 to dbl. EP; MC, V
Victorian Mansion Guest House, The, 8; Rates: $18 dbl. EP
Virginian Hotel, 163; Rates: $20 to $50 dbl. EP; MC, V
White Gull Inn, 63; Rates: $30 to $40 dbl. EP
Whittmond Hotel, 1; call for current rates
Ye English Inn, 89; Rates: $14 to $20 dbl. EP; MC, V

THE COMPLEAT TRAVELER'S READER REPORT

To: *The Compleat Traveler*
    c/o Burt Franklin & Co., Inc.
    235 East 44th Street
    New York, New York 10017 U.S.A.

Dear Compleat Traveler:

I have used your book in _____ (country or region).
I would like to offer the following ☐ new recommendation, ☐ comment,
☐ suggestion, ☐ criticism, ☐ or complaint about:

Name of Country Inn or Hotel:

_____

Address: _____

_____

Comments:

Day of my visit: _____   Length of stay: _____

From (name): _____

Address _____

_____ Telephone: _____